Inside Christian Community

ROSINE HAMMETT, C.S.C.
LOUGHLAN SOFIELD, S.T.

ISBN 0-929754-00-X
Printed in the United States of America.

Throughout this book we have been careful to protect the anonymity of specific communities and persons except when permission was given to do otherwise.

Sister Rosine Hammett is a member of the Congregation of the Sisters of the Holy Cross of Notre Dame, Indiana. She is currently assistant director of the Washington Archdiocesan Consultation Center as well as assistant director of the Center for Religion and Psychiatry in Washington, D.C. As lecturer, communications consultant, therapist, and facilitator of personal growth experiences, she has worked with both men and women religious in the United States, Brazil, and Bangladesh. She also teaches group pastoral ministry at the Washington Theological Union in Silver Spring, Maryland.

Brother Loughlan Sofield is a member of the Missionary Servants of the Most Holy Trinity. Currently he is co-director of the Ministries Center for the Laity. In the past he has been director of the Washington Archdiocesan Consultation Center and assistant director of the Center for Religion and Psychiatry in Washington, D.C. For the last ten years his primary ministry has been to ministers in the United States, Europe, and Australia.

TO
D'AG
A friend, teacher, role model, and benefactor—a man
with a vision of religious life and ministry who was willing to
train us, encourage us, and enable us to use our gifts
to minister to others in ministry

Contents

Foreword

As a former teacher of Brother Loughlan and Sister Rosine, I must admit to the great sense of pride I felt as I read the beautiful insights their work contains. They have clarified so many valuable and too often misunderstood truths about the multifaceted vagaries of our natures—the psychological and behavioral manifestations of basic needs, the necessity for effective communication within communities that results in personal growth for each member—and they have brought it all together and have shown the way out of the trenches of disappointment, dejection—yes, even despair. This work is a most effective solace and resource for those who have experienced or may be experiencing the emptiness and loneliness that too often exists within community.

Thanks to the Holy Spirit working through the person of Pope John XXIII, the Second Vatican Council convened and brought sweeping changes in both the structure and the practice of Catholicism. One significant development is the shift in theological emphasis from a so-called vertical relationship with God to a more horizontal one, which finds God in social dimensions as well. This new emphasis underscores the need for a vision of the Church as "the people of God." The Church is the Body of Christ, and it is through the Church that we fulfill our spiritual destinies. But the Church is also a group, and in our religious practices we are well aware that the Sacraments, the liturgy, even the Scriptures become so much more meaningful when seen and used as a group function.

Modern psychology, which provided us with tools for understanding the human psyche, has now given us the ability to comprehend the dynamics of groups. The Church, although guided in a unique way by the Holy Spirit, is subject to the psychological laws that pertain to any human group, laws that are inexorable and constantly at work, to be lifted only by Divine intervention. To further the life of the Church, it is useful to apply the principles of group dynamics. When the forces governed by these laws are recognized, they can be productively channeled. When they are ignored or misunderstood, they can be counterproductive, or even destructive.

We now realize that religious communities consist of distinct individuals whose interaction can be a productive and gratifying growth experience—or quite the contrary. The forces that determine the type of experience are a function of grace and of individual psychologies responding to that grace. A better understanding of group dynamics can reverse a group heading in a negative direction and point it toward a more positive goal.

With the ever increasing demands on so few available clergy and vowed religious, the Church's effectiveness must be multiplied if it is to flourish. One way of bringing this about is through a group approach, in which laymen, laywomen, and religious perform valuable services to churches and allied groups. In addition, the group approach is a powerful instrument for ecumenical progress, bringing together beneficiaries from disparate churches, both as group members and as group leaders.

Now for a bit of history. In the late 1960s the Center for Religion and Psychiatry took shape as a unit of the Washington Psychiatric Institute Foundation (WPI), based mainly in the clinical setting of the WPI. With the birth of the Washington Theological Coalition (now the Washington Theological Union), our activities were situated in the academic atmosphere of the seminary. The goal of the center was to acquaint seminarians and others in ministry with the principles of group dynamics and to relate these principles to any church-related function. This has been achieved to a creditable degree over the past decade, and now students include vowed religious and lay persons of many faiths and occupations. Their common denominator is that they have acquired the knowledge and the ability to form groups and to maintain them until their goals are achieved. Two outstanding students—both of whom contributed significantly to the growth and development of the center—are the authors of this book. At different times both have been the education director and the associate director of the center. I doubt that the center could have flourished as it has without their dedicated and talented involvement.

In closing, I invite you readers to consider the remarkable action of grace working through your efforts as you offer the fruits of your labor for the coming of the Kingdom. May the Father's love continue to draw you onward, the Son's compassion and peace ever enfold you, and the Spirit's wisdom constantly inspire you.

Angelo D'Agostino, S.J., M.D.

Acknowledgments

Since this book focuses on the understanding of group dynamics as they affect community living, and since we are convinced of the value of group living, it is noteworthy that this book is the result of the combined effort of many people, a group.

We are deeply indebted to the following friends for their kindness and patience in reading the manuscript and offering suggestions and advice drawn from their own varied experiences: William Burkert, S.T.; Dorothy Anne Cahill, C.S.C.; Emeline Cunningham, C.S.C.; Henry Hammett, S.J.; Brenda Hermann, M.S.B.T.; Carroll Juliano, S.H.C.J.; Olivia Marie Hutchison, C.S.C.; Paul Michalenko, S.T.; Denise Renaud, R.J.M.; George Carlin; Malachy Sofield, S.T.; and Mae Sofield.

Rosemarie Melillo, Loretta Marie Valdes, C.S.C., and Eileen Cleverly were indefatigable in their willingness to do all the tedious clerical tasks, as was Francis Xavier Regan, C.S.C., who typed the manuscript.

Denise Renaud, R.J.M., contributed greatly to the development of the material in Chapter 6. Carroll Juliano, S.H.C.J., was invaluable in the assistance she provided in the writing of some of the material for Chapter 2.

We owe a deep and loving debt of gratitude to James J. Gill, S.J., M.D., and Linda Amadeo. In addition to their encouragement and support, they have continually shared their expertise and skills with us, helping us to grow in our own personal, ministerial, and professional lives.

There is no way we could adequately express our appreciation to Joan Rodriguez for the consistent and professional editing she so graciously did during the long development of this book.

Finally, we are deeply indebted to the communities and individuals who have shared their lives with us and allowed us to be present with them in their struggles and joys of building effective communities. It is their encouragement that has provided the necessary stimulus to continue with the book when our enthusiasm waned.

Introduction

Community life, life within a group, is intended to provide support for emotional, psychological, spiritual, and apostolic growth. This is the ideal. The reality, as those of us who have lived in religious community know, often falls far short of this. Community living can become painful and complex in a way the good Lord never intended it to be. In this book we share some insights into group dynamics as they affect our efforts to grow as faith communities.

We begin by defining our basic terms, since they are subject to many and varied interpretations:

Group. A group is a collection of individuals who interact and interrelate in a face-to-face manner around a common goal. They remain in relationship with one another long enough to influence one another, establish clear identification of membership, and act in a unified manner.

Religious Community. A religious community is a group whose common goal is to live and spread the gospel. Membership consists of individuals who believe they have been called to live with others with a similar call. Community is not an end in itself but rather a life-style to support, nourish, and challenge the members to live the gospel more fully.

Dynamics. Dynamics are the forces operating within a group that influence what occurs in that group. They refer to the interrelationships among members as well as to the interrelationships between member and external forces.

While our focus is on religious community, the theories presented should be of value to anyone working with or in a group setting, e.g., a team, a staff, an advisory board. Our approach in each chapter is to describe the group dynamic, to relate this dynamic more specifically to community living, and to provide some suggestions about what can be done to maximize the positive potential of this dynamic.

In Chapter 1 we discuss the value of community and our assumptions about community living. Chapter 2 outlines a model for understanding the stages through which communities grow. Chapter 3 brings together some research on groups and highlights the particular dynamics that have special relevance to community living. Chapters 4 and 5 focus on communication: Chapter 4 presents a general overview of concepts of communication basic to facilitating the development of community, and Chapter 5 describes more specific skills of communication such as listening, dialoguing, and confrontation. Chapter 6 has a twofold goal: It is intended to help anyone facilitating community groups; more important, it is also directed toward teaching communities to be better consumers through *knowledgeable* use of outside facilitators. Chapter 7 offers some concrete ideas for action, individual and corporate, to improve the quality of life in community.

GOALS FOR THE BOOK

There are a number of goals that prompted us to write this book. Some of these are:

1. To provide ways to overcome the obstacles that frustrate religious who desire to share their lives with others in a truly radical and evangelical spirit.

2. To facilitate a better integration of the human dimension of religious' lives in community so as to facilitate their growth in their faith and service commitment.

3. To clarify and minimize the frustrations religious encounter in trying to live and work together with other good, sincere, committed, holy people.

4. To help religious who are experiencing pain and frustration in adapting to the changing structures of community life feel a greater sense of peace and security.

5. To aid religious in obtaining greater support from the persons they are living with in community.

6. To enhance community meetings so that they are sources of real opportunities for spiritual and emotional growth for individuals and communities.

7. To build communities that are groups with whom we can share our successes and failures, joys and sorrows, fears and hopes, and anything else that assists us in our growth to becoming the people God has called us to be.

There are a few questions you should keep in mind as you read this book. Have you experienced the dynamics we describe in your community? What might these dynamics be saying to you? What can you do now in your present local community to improve the quality of life?

I

Putting The Scene in Focus

A cartoon caught our attention recently. Two young boys are in a library. One of them comments excitedly on the great "how-to" books he is finding. The second replies somewhat cynically, "I'm looking for the 'why-bother' books."

As we struggled to complete this book in the midst of hundreds of other pressing demands, we asked ourselves that same question, "Why bother?" Our answer grew from a personal conviction that people in full-time ministry need to experience supportive community to be effective ministers.

For a number of years we taught group dynamics, supervised others working with groups, and spent countless hours facilitating groups. Much of this work has been with communities. We feel the resultant knowledge and insights, if shared, can be helpful to others striving to better the quality of community life.

The incident that provided the impetus for writing this book was a casual comment made by a woman religious during a workshop we were conducting. She mentioned that it was strange that her early formation in religious life prepared her for so many things—how to pray, how to live the vows, approaches to being an effective apostle—but there had been no preparation or training for living in community. It was assumed this was unnecessary.

The truth of this statement struck us; our reflections on our own initial formation confirmed it. From that chance comment came the incentive we needed "to bother."

WHAT YOU WILL NOT FIND IN THIS BOOK

Before we share with you what you can expect to find in this book, we feel it is important to clarify what you will not find.

We are not attempting to offer a theology of community; other persons far more capable have done this in other works. If you feel frustrated at times because the underpinnings of theological understanding of community seem to be absent, recall that our purpose is to deal with the group element of community rather than with the faith and service dimensions. This in no way questions the paramount importance of theology in our call to community. To the contrary, group theory and dynamics are certainly not going to bring disparate persons into improved communications when religious values are not shared. Faith, however, does not negate the importance of communication skills that serve to foster human development and so prepare for a union of hearts in a true community. Building community, or communion in the Lord, is the work of the Lord, but human hands and human knowledge of techniques can assist.

WHAT YOU WILL FIND IN THIS BOOK

The primary focus of this book is to describe group dynamics as they manifest themselves in community living. We intend to deal with the group process, focusing directly on the problem of how to make community groups function more smoothly. No magic potion can be used to become more sensitive and effective in group interaction. Lists of techniques and "how-to's" may be effective to some extent, but anyone working with groups soon becomes aware that in the area of human relations the skills of group interaction come with experience. These skills, however, can be acquired faster and applied more easily when they are based on knowledge and insight.

WHY BOTHER

Is there value in community living? Perhaps raising such a question borders on heresy or cynicism, but we feel compelled to ask it. Our experience has been that most members of religious communities are emphatic in answering "Yes." However, if values can be deduced from behavior, the daily lives of many religious give little evidence of their beliefs, and doubts should certainly be raised. The truth probably is that most of us are ambivalent. But this is not often faced, and therefore, it can't be dealt with. We want the support, the caring, the affirming that community can provide. Yet, we fear that we might have to change some familiar patterns of living or set limitations on ourselves if our community is to be truly of value. Many things make community unattractive; only a conviction that we are called by God can make it reasonable.

One way of reducing ambivalence is to look at both the positive and the negative aspects of community life. Only when we can demythologize community and objectify our ambivalence are we free to embrace and commit ourselves to living community in such a way that it is truly of value and a source of growth.

In other chapters, we will deal with some of the dynamics that make community life difficult. Here we shall discuss four reasons why it is essential to improve the quality of community life.

As Christians we are called to a life of community. Since Vatican II the Church has placed greater emphasis on the communal aspect of God's call to His people. Changes in both sacramental and liturgical forms indicate this renewed emphasis. For example, the sacraments of baptism and confirmation have new rites that emphasize their communal nature. The focus has shifted from the passive role of the recipient to what Pope Paul VI in his apostolic exhortation *On Evangelization in the Modern World* called living the sacrament.[1] Similar changes are taking place in the rites for other sacraments and for the liturgy.

Our salvation, sanctification, and reconciliation occur within the context of the Christian community. God calls us to minister and spread His Kingdom through the community in which we find ourselves.

Community is a sign of hope and a witness to a secular world.

In *Pursuit of Loneliness*, Philip Slater sketches a picture of society in which the basic desires of human beings to share and live in trust and cooperation with one another are frustrated.[2] In a world beset by these frustrations, people need to see a group of persons, motivated by the gospel and their love of God, who live in such a way that loneliness and alienation are dispelled. They need a corporate witness to the fact that these conditions can be alleviated if we live a life founded on belief in the Lord Jesus. By virtue of our profession, our lives must proclaim Jesus' love for His people. Communication through deed is the essence of Christian presence and the true sign of hope for others.

Jesus, in His discourse at the Last Supper, called upon the community to be the truest sign to future generations that He had been sent by His Father into the world. "Father, may they be one in Us, as You are in Me and I in You, so that the world may believe it was You Who sent Me." (John 17:21)

The unity of His followers is the proof of Jesus' presence in the world. In responding to the Lord's special call to religious life, we have made a commitment to witness and to proclaim the good news of the Kingdom of God.

While addressing all Christians, the document *On Evangelization in the Modern World* makes a special demand on religious to give wordless witness, through their lives in loving community, of the love of the Father in sending His Son into the world.[3] Those who proclaim the good news must demonstrate the life-giving power of the message through their own lives. We must begin working to live community in a manner befitting our public profession, otherwise we must cease to preach it as a Christian ideal for others.

Community provides opportunity for growth and maturing. Religious community life has a pragmatic value. It can be a force for spiritual, personal, and ministerial growth and maturity for its members. It is not the only source, but it is one source, a powerful one, helping us grow. In therapy and counseling we have seen hurting priests and religious who were unable or unwilling to take advantage of the resources they had in community. They were almost destroyed when help was only an arm's length away. Although we have seen very few psychologically sick priests and religious, we have encountered many hurting, pained, scared, and lonely people whose condition was due to their inability or unwillingness to use the resources of their local community.

If God is calling us to live in community, He must have placed within community the gifts and graces needed for the growth of its members. He would not call us to do the impossible—to enter into a life-style that frustrates our growth in relation to Him.

We must develop a climate in which persons in community can maximize their potential for spiritual and psychological growth. We believe that the human dimensions of religious life can be vastly improved through knowledge of the processes at work in community living. Building community, or communion in the Lord, is the work of the Lord, and an act of faith is required of a group of individuals who want to grow together in the Lord in the face of everyday experiences of their separateness.

Unless the quality of community life improves, there will be another large exodus from religious life. Many religious greeted the changes after Vatican II with great optimism. There was promise of a new style of community living that emphasized the human

REASONS FOR IMPROVING THE QUALITY OF COMMUNITY LIFE
As Christians we are called to a life of community.
Community is a sign of hope and a witness to a secular world.
Community provides opportunity for growth and maturing.
Unless the quality of community life improves, there will be another large exodus from religious life.

dimension of life in community. Many religious felt revitalized by the emphasis on a communal life with greater intimacy and better relationships among those living it. The decade and a half that has passed since the close of that council have seen many changes, but many religious feel that these have been superficial and have not brought about the hoped for improvements. Some people have left because they lost confidence that community could foster their growth. Few of these people can be labeled malcontents. They are people of integrity who felt forced to leave because the experience of community life was draining them psychologically, emotionally, spiritually, and apostolically. Unfortunately this trend will continue unless some sign of hope reverses it.

ASSUMPTIONS ABOUT COMMUNITIES

Through our work with communities of men and women religious, we have arrived at certain assumptions that form the basis for our belief that religious community living can be benefited by a better understanding of the dynamics and processes operating in any group.

1. Communities are groups; therefore, the dynamics that occur in any group also occur in communities.

2. Groups are powerful agents of change. This change may result in positive or negative consequences. A group may move in such a way that every member experiences growth, or the group may exercise a destructive influence. Early theorists recognized both possibilities. Sigmund Freud could conceive of a group only as a mob capable of great acts of unbridled violence.[4] He compared groups to violent, destructive animals. Carl Jung, a contemporary of Freud, had a view that was not much more attractive. He declared: "When a hundred clever heads join in a group, one big nincompoop is the result because every individual is trammeled by the otherness of the others."[5] Psychologist Fritz Redl has recently commented: "You can bring together five or six healthy people and still end up with a sick group."[6]

Recent studies of groups and a better understanding of their dynamics have produced more positive attitudes toward group behavior and the power of groups as constructive forces. In *Psy-*

ASSUMPTIONS ABOUT COMMUNITIES

Communities are groups; therefore, the dynamics that occur in any group also occur in communities.

Groups are powerful agents of change.

The extent to which we understand and use the dynamics operating in a community can influence it toward productive or destructive behavior.

God has called us to community, and in community He reveals Himself to us.

Community groups are unique inasmuch as they are hybrids. They share various traits with other groups such as families, peer groups, and support groups.

As persons attempt to meet their needs in community, problems arise, tensions develop, emotions come into play, and group goals conflict with individual goals.

The group is an inextricable part of the human condition. At all stages of our lives, we need to belong to groups.

chodynamics of Family Life, family therapist Nathan Ackerman states: "To keep one's health, one must continuously share it with other healthy persons. One must find a group climate in which one can continue to grow and actualize one's potentialities in healthy human relationships."[7] Angelo D'Agostino, a priest-psychoanalyst, says, "Theologically speaking, we are saved and healed in a Christian community of love—a transcendent group. It behooves the pastoral minister to understand the underlying dynamics of groups to be able to channel their energies, with grace, to constructive, healing ends."[8]

3. *The extent to which we understand and use the dynamics operating in a community can influence it toward productive or destructive behavior*. When we understand the dynamics, we can ensure that communities are what they are meant to be, true support groups for people engaged in growing in their relationships with the Lord and using their gifts in ministry to further His Kingdom. If we do not understand the dynamics, we will probably experience communities that do not help us to grow in this relationship and ministry but rather militate against it. Don Brophy, managing editor of the Paulist Press, observed that each prayer group he belonged to had ended in erosion because no one in the groups understood the dynamics operating.[9] We believe that the same thing is true of community living. Most communities never achieve their full potential because their members don't understand the dynamics that can undermine the group.

Systems (groups) therapists believe that problems do not originate in the individual. They originate in systems and therefore help must be directed toward the interpersonal relationships or difficulties creating the problem.

4. *God has called us to community, and in community He reveals Himself to us*. The individual call has always been a call to share with others. The foundation of community life is a commitment. It is a special relationship between persons who agree to take on a mutual responsibility for one another's lives in common relationship to Jesus as Lord. Each of us, responding to a call to the fullness of life in Christ, feels a need to join others with the same goal. We believe that we can be more faithful to this call in collaboration with others.

5. *Community groups are unique inasmuch as they are hybrids; nevertheless, they still follow the usual group processes.* They share various traits with other groups such as families, peer groups, and support groups. The difference lies in how the group dynamics must be responded to in community to facilitate its growth potential. Later chapters will focus on aspects of groups that can help explain the dynamics operating in community and how understanding these dynamics can be used to advantage by the members.

6. *As persons attempt to meet their needs in community, problems arise, tensions develop, emotions come into play, and group goals conflict with individual goals.* Just as in individual behavior nothing happens by chance, in group behavior a complexity of forces operates to cause the group to act. We should not be surprised to find tension and frustration when a diverse group of people attempt to live together in a closely bound community. To expect otherwise is unrealistic.

7. *The group is an inextricable part of the human condition. At all stages of our lives, we need to belong to groups.* We are born into the family group and throughout our lives we can never exist in isolation. The quality of our lives depends on the effectiveness of our group relations.

As persons become familiar with the dynamics of group interaction, they begin to understand why groups can be both frustrating and rewarding experiences. Learning these dynamics is probably the best way to further personal growth and to achieve greater enjoyment in group participation.

NOTES

1. Pope Paul VI, "Evangelization in the Modern World," *Evangelization Today*, (Northport, N.Y.: Costello, 1977), p. 23, #47.
2. Philip Slater, *The Pursuit of Loneliness*, (Boston: Beacon Press 1970), p. 5.
3. Pope Paul VI, *"Evangelization,"* p. 37f., #69.
4. Sigmund Freud, *Group Psychology and the Analysis of the Ego* (New York: W.W. Norton & Co., Inc., 1959), p. 54.

5. Fritz Redl, "The Impact of the Group Process and the Problem of Clinical Caution," Thirtieth Annual Conference of the American Group Psychotherapy Association, Inc., Detroit, Michigan, February 7, 1973.

6. Redl, "The Impact of the Group Process."

7. Nathan Ackerman, *Psychodynamics of Family Life* (New York: Basic Books, Inc., 1958), p. xii.

8. Angelo D'Agostino, *Bulletin for the Center for Religion and Psychiatry Pastoral Group Leadership Program.* 1979–80.

9. Don Brophy, "Why I Don't Pray Anymore," *National Catholic Reporter,* March 1, 1974.

II

Stages in the Development of Community

A community is always changing, becoming, interacting, and reacting. This movement is characteristic of all groups and usually happens on an unconscious level. One way of looking at this dynamic change is to identify the stages through which groups pass. All groups go through fairly predictable stages, and local religious communities are no exception. Certain progressions take place as people grow in their relationships with one another.

When we use the term stage, we are talking about steps that one goes through in a developmental process. Psychologists such as Erik Erikson have helped us to understand human behavior by looking at the development of a human being as proceeding through stages from birth to death.[1] Similarly, by delineating various stages through which groups proceed from incorporation to termination, social scientists have helped us to understand the operation and dynamics of groups.

Nevertheless, it must be remembered that describing stages in any theoretical formulation, whether these are related to the individual, group, or parish, is artificial. The reality is never as clear-cut as it appears on paper. Stages must always be viewed as helpful guides, never as definitive facts.

This chapter will describe the stages in the development of a community. After having worked with dozens of local communities, and having drawn from many models, we have adapted a particular model of stages based on our observations and reflections. We will first present some general observations about stages.

Understanding stages through which communities progress is important for a number of reasons, including the following:

• It allows us to identify where a community is developmentally at any given time. Having identified this, it is much easier to determine what must be done to achieve the next stage of development. Too often we want to see the community at an ideal point. The frustration of many people in community comes from the fact that the community is not where the members would like it to be. They attempt to move rapidly from where they are to where they would like to be without going through the slow process of moving from stage to stage. It is impossible to skip stages, and attempting to do so will only lead to frustration.

• Realizing that stages are universal and that all groups pass through them often helps to relieve some of the anxiety felt by community members. Too often members live with a host of "shoulds." "We should have a community free of conflict. Everyone should love everyone else." The truth, we believe, is that "You shouldn't 'should' yourself!" As people begin to realize that their group experience is a part of normal and necessary development, their anxiety and sense of failure may be reduced. Group members are then ready to view each stage as part of the ordinary process of group development.

• Once people are aware of the stages, they are able to name what they are experiencing, thereby making it less frightening. Once an experience has been named, the members can communicate about their experiences more easily. However, communities have often put too much hope in communication techniques. These can be helpful but are of limited value in the long run. Techniques such as paraphrasing and active listening become mechanistic unless the people involved also comprehend what is happening in the group. Understanding the dynamics will free people to communicate more openly and honestly.

Four characteristics of stages must be kept in mind: stages are artificial; stages usually overlap; a community can become fixated at any stage; and communities can regress to an earlier stage. Usually a community will be in a number of stages at any given time, but by analyzing the situation, it should become apparent that one stage is predominant. We are dealing with a human situation, and no two humans are ever at precisely the same point of development. Therefore, we should not expect all the members of a community to be at exactly the same stage. Acknowledging this, we can, however, get a clearer perception of where the community is as a whole.

The model we have developed perceives local communities as moving through eight stages: (1) orientation, (2) inclusion, (3) control, (4) conflict, (5) cohesion, (6) faith sharing, (7) intimacy, and (8) termination. We will describe the normal dynamic as it occurs in any group, indicate how this is expressed in community, and offer suggestions for helping the group move to the next stage. An outline of this model can be found on page 14.

Most of the communities we have worked with have encountered greatest difficulty at three stages: conflict, intimacy, and termination. Therefore we have devoted more time to these three phases.

STAGE 1: ORIENTATION

The initial stage of a group involves orientation. The members tentatively try out their wings. They seek to discover what norms are acceptable and unacceptable within the group. They search for structure and goals. There is a great dependency on the member who seems to be leading and a lot of concern about group boundaries.

At the first meeting of any group, most members tend to feel inadequate, although they don't want to show it. There is a tendency to be watchful and careful about what is revealed. Members size up one another and try to make themselves more comfortable by stereotyping others. To feel better about themselves, they may, for instance, tell themselves that this group is much less people oriented than the group they just left. It is only after the initial probings that guards are dropped and individuals can

STAGES OF COMMUNITY GROUPS

STAGE	PREDOMINANT FEELING	HOW THE FEELING IS EXPRESSED	WHAT YOU CAN DO
1. Orientation	Insecurity	Talking Getting clarity Silence Questioning whether this group meets my needs	Clarify norms, expectations, etc.
2. Inclusion	Fear of exclusion	Do I belong? Will I be accepted? Am I different? Fear of doing something that will get me rejected	Find ways of including everyone Encourage asking questions
3. Control	Competitiveness	How can I be important in this group? Who is most important? Why?	Focus on the unique value of each person Decrease differences Focus on commonality
4. Conflict	Tension	Fight Nonattendance Regression Denial of the problem	Raise the conflict issue and deal with it
5. Cohesion	Relaxation	Lots of interaction Concern for one another Accomplishment of tasks	Make sure the group is moving toward its purpose
6. Faith Sharing	Peacefulness	Honest sharing Trust	Make sure people feel comfortable
7. Intimacy	Ambivalence	How close do I want to get to these people? Approach-avoidance	Discover a comfortable level without feeling guilty
8. Termination	Avoidance	Attempt to avoid the end	Deal with your feelings

begin to establish personal roles and reveal more characteristic behaviors. Then each person can be seen as a unique individual and the differences can be tolerated, even appreciated.

In the very early stages, groups are often a source of anxiety and discomfort. The degree of anxiety is diminished as relationships deepen and the time spent together increases. However, with rare exceptions, people never feel as comfortable in a group as they do with one person.

Each person, overtly or covertly, anticipates rejection by the group. There is constantly some fear of being slighted, criticized, attacked, or humiliated. In communities, this fear expresses itself in diverse ways. It may be communicated through silence, defensiveness, or any of the many ways we characteristically deal with fear. The community usually spends most of its time attempting to clarify what behavior is acceptable. Meetings may be characterized by either long periods of superficial chatter or periods of silence. In either case, the goal is the same: to discern who the other people are as individuals and as a group and who appears to be a potential ally or enemy.

This stage is a relatively short one. If community members are clear about their expectations regarding other members, and if they have established norms that they feel are important for the maintenance of the community, they should spell these out at this stage. What are the expectations of each member regarding prayer life, presence, inclusion of noncommunity members, responsibilities for the maintenance of the house, etc.? These expectations should not be handed down as dictums but rather proposed as the norms and expectations. If these guided the community during the previous year, they should be discussed and renegotiated, since anytime membership changes, a new group is formed and consequently there is a need to determine norms and collective expectations.

STAGE 2: INCLUSION

The group then enters into a second stage, inclusion-exclusion. The transition to this stage happens at an unconscious level. Members begin to sort out those who are "in" and those who are "out." Such distinctions may be made on the basis of new members versus old members. New members are made to feel outside the group when old members discuss people and situations they alone are familiar with. Usually, suggestions by newer members are met with "We've never done it that way before," an attitude that seems to pervade this stage. Unless new members are assertive, they will find themselves excluded from much of the ordinary dialogue going on in the house and begin to experience a sense of loneliness. Feelings associated with termination of a previous mission will likely be felt more acutely now. Those who feel "in" need to practice a greater Christian sensitivity to what others might be experiencing. This is especially true in light of Freud's theory that when individuals are excluded from a group, they are compelled to replace group formations with neurotic formations.[2] People who feel that the group excludes them and cannot meet their needs may revert to neurotic behavior to attain this need satisfaction. They may act out in self-destructive ways, such as alcohol abuse or bizarre behavior, to force a response from the group.

Other separations in communities may be made on the basis of conservative versus liberal or on apostolate versus apostolate. Members begin to ask questions: Who am I in this group? How effective am I? How effective can I be? Does my being here make a difference? Will any of my needs be met? Where is this community going? Is this where I want to go? How much can I afford to risk with this group?

If the group is to move beyond this stage, it must establish a climate of safety in which those who are feeling alienated are able to ask questions that will help them to feel more like members of the group.

STAGE 3: CONTROL

The next stage begins almost simultaneously with stage 2. This is the "up-down" stage, the period during which the group establishes a hierarchy among its members. Power is the key ingredient in almost all human relationships. Members test out their influence in the group, usually at a subtle or unconscious level. Status may be established by different criteria, but the membership usually arranges itself on a continuum of least important to most important. For example, criteria may include academic degrees, age, verbal ability, progressive attitude, or conservative attitude. Competition is fierce, and the threat to each person's sense of self-worth is great. Questions begin to arise: How much can I influence this group? Who will influence me? How much am I willing to be influenced and by whom? Members will carefully assess the situation before they enter into a relationship with the group.

At this stage it is important that every member experience a sense of personal value in the group. If they don't, they tend to drop out, that is, while still formally remaining part of the community, they will exist as far on the periphery as possible, consciously determined to remain physically and emotionally detached from the community.

STAGE 4: CONFLICT

A group cannot become cohesive until it is able to deal with conflict, which is or can be a positive experience. Conflict can arise because (1) group members are so bound together that their actions negatively affect one another; (2) each member has different needs and values; and (3) decisions essential to the group's continuation are faced. Because there is concern about the group as a whole, members are often willing to sacrifice a great deal to improve the situation. Sometimes, rather than accept their differences, members allow themselves to be taken over by a leader and for a sense of false peace give up their individual responsibility for the group. Many decisions are simply evaded.

Conflict is an extremely difficult issue for most people living in community. Many never learned how to handle it and often see it as wrong or give it an importance far beyond its potential. At this stage some communities become stuck. Tensions develop. If a community is unable or unwilling to deal with conflict, it can never go on to the stage of becoming a true faith community. Conflict is necessary—without it the group will not grow. Members must develop the ability to confront one another.

Conflict is productive only when it is resolved. Unresolved, it hangs like a dark cloud over the group. In communities we have worked with, it has been likened to a time bomb placed in the middle of the room waiting to explode. Too often the major theme in the community at this point is peace at any price. However, the conflict will not evaporate by simply wishing it to do so. It has to be confronted. Every community we have worked with has been able to deal effectively with conflict once the attempt has been made. It is not the conflict but the fear of conflict that is destructive.

Conflict is a natural and desirable part of human interaction at both the individual and the group level. When dealt with, it reduces the natural tension and frustration people experience as they work together; it allows for the expression of aggressive feelings that could otherwise interfere with the quality of the group's work; and it is inevitable if the members are truly involved. Unfortunately, most communities feel they are incapable of dealing with conflict and go to great lengths to avoid it. Yet there is increasing evidence that conflict handled constructively is an important element in overcoming the sense of alienation people experience today, not only in religious communities but in other groups as well.

Conflict must be raised, looked at squarely, and dealt with. How we deal with it is also important. In his research Irving Yalom discovered that the most beneficial groups were those in which members interacted in a "confrontive, forthright, non-defensive, non-judgmental manner."[3]

In dealing with conflict, the group begins to get a sense of its own potency. Often the healthiest communities bring in facilitators to help them through this stage; they recognize that the stage is essential to their successful union.

STAGE 5: COHESION

When a community has begun to deal effectively with conflict, it moves into the stage of cohesiveness, defined as the ability of the group to stick together. Another term for this quality might be group loyalty. A highly cohesive group is one in which members work for the good of the group. Cohesive groups are more productive, have a higher morale, and have better communication than groups with little cohesiveness. In a cohesive group, the members take the initiative; they distribute work loads and take up the slack in time of stress. In groups with little cohesiveness, the members tend to wait to be told what to do.

During the cohesive stage things are relatively calm. Rapport among the members is usually good, and members are able to address themselves to working at common goals and aims. During this period the group members feel good about themselves and reveal a sense of trust in and joy with one another. Release from the tension of conflict seems to free the energy of the group to address itself to creative tasks, insights, and performance. The members show a greater sharing and tolerance and are more effective at decision making. They have a sense of growth. Pursuit of personal goals does not detract from the handling of the group's tasks. Members feel responsible for the success of the group. Interpersonal and group maintenance issues are likely to receive greater attention because of the implicit need to guard against sheer conformity, dominance, withdrawal, and other self-centered behaviors that may seriously deter the achievement of commitment. The group experiences enough tension to want to change, and they have faith in their ability to cope with their tensions since they have done so before.

The problem with group cohesiveness is that members like sweetness and light and may suppress their hostility so that they can remain at this level. But this would be contrary to what characterizes a truly cohesive group. In his study of groups, Yalom stated: "We must not mistakenly equate cohesiveness with comfort. Although cohesive groups may show greater acceptance, intimacy, and understanding, there is evidence that they also permit greater development and expression of hostility and conflict."[4] Communities sometimes erroneously feel they have achieved their goals when they arrive at this stage; people are beginning to truly understand one another, see one another more clearly as gifted people, and take time to do things together more spontaneously. Community prayer becomes much easier at this point.

Most people come to community for the sake of mission. The struggle to achieve a sense of strong community has often been so frustrating and painful that there is a tendency toward a nesting in community. At this point the task of communities is to focus more outwardly and to begin serious corporate reflection on the ministries in which they are engaged. Members must be prepared to discuss their ministries more openly and honestly and to be ready to challenge one another to grow in their apostolic zeal.

STAGE 6: FAITH SHARING

While community members have spent a great deal of time in earlier stages talking about the values of sharing faith and prayer, they now come to a stage at which they can actually begin to share faith openly and directly. By faith sharing, we mean more than just a group of people coming together to say the same prayers at the same time in the same room. We are talking about the ability to really share with one another the answer to such questions as Who is my God? and How do I experience Him in my life? Faith and religious experiences are gifts of God, and these are given for the sake of the community, not just the individual. The striking thing about this stage is the ambivalence community members feel about it. Most community groups have long, very honest, and very sincere discussions on the values members place on sharing faith or prayers. However, somehow the actual faith sharing is neglected. We have a responsibility to share these gifts but are often reluctant to do so. Since faith and religious experiences are gifts, we will be held responsible for how we used them, not how we enjoyed them.

An interesting phenomenon related to faith sharing is that when it finally happens, it is often followed by a period of conflict or distancing. In our initial work with religious communities, we expected that it would be followed by a time of peace, but this has not been our experience. We have developed two theories that might account for this. The first is that having shared very intimate details of their lives, people realize how vulnerable they have become and hide behind the mask of conflict or distance for protection. The second is that having shared at the level of faith, people develop a new trust and an openness that free them to deal with conflicts that have been suppressed.

Since resistance and fear of vulnerability operate to keep a person from actually sharing faith or prayer, breaking down these defenses frees us to deal with or confront what we could not handle before. Bringing in a retreat director or someone from outside who can help the community at this stage of sharing can be a good way to move the group from the resistance and fear of vulnerability to the accomplishment of this stage.

STAGE 7: INTIMACY

Although intimacy is present as an issue at each stage of development, it becomes a special issue at this point. Members of the group are faced with the question of how close they really want to get to one another. They often experience a sense of ambivalence, anxiety, and discomfort. We have an urge to share our true feelings, but we fear that by doing so we will make ourselves vulnerable and will be rejected or criticized. The questions for each person are: Can I trust these people? How far can I trust them? Do I really want to trust them? Will they keep my confidence? Is it worth the investment of myself that intimacy requires?

Intimacy is probably the most stressful of all human experiences. It reveals a capacity to share with others our deepest joys, aspirations, anxieties, and problems. In an intimate relationship we are called to step out from behind our facades and expose ourselves in the nakedness of our limitations, weaknesses, and poverties. It means allowing another to know of our doubts about ourselves and our own worth. It means letting others see us as we are and not as we would like them to see us.

To do this requires a great deal of love and trust—not only expressed by the other person but also by ourselves. The risk and vulnerability entailed can only be sustained if we are self-accepting. As we open ourselves to others, we are in effect saying, "Here I am, trusting and defenseless before you." The ability to risk this openness presumes that we have had other persons in our lives with whom we had intimate relationships. Through their affirmation we have learned to be comfortable while being open and trusting.

Often the traditional culture in which we grew up taught us to avoid intimacy. We did not express our feelings openly, and we kept a respectful distance toward authority figures and toward our elders.

Contrary to this, today's popular literature and media encourage instant intimacy. Cocktail parties have their goblet conversations, first-name strangers, and animated and superficial chit-chat that never allow another to get near. In truth, there is no instant intimacy. Intimacy requires a great deal of love and a willingness to receive other persons as they are and to trust that we may be received in the same way. In intimate relationships one person is not absorbed by the other, identities are not compromised. Nor is there an attempt to manage or manipulate others for one's own advantage.

Intimacy frightens the nonaffirmed person, the one who rarely receives praise for anything. Out of fear these persons look for a place apart where they wait in loneliness for someone to seek them out. Unfortunately, there seem to be more hiders than seekers. The hiders wait in vain to be found.

Living in community forces us to deal with the issue of intimacy. We cannot ignore it. When intimacy is a reality in community, persons mature. When it is resisted or denied as an issue, persons will feel isolated. The ability to enter into relationships of intimacy and mutuality opens the way to experiences in which the self expands beyond its own limitations in depths of feeling, understanding, and insight. Our identities are strengthened by what we mean to other persons we respect. Without others it is difficult to know our own boundaries. To be without others raises the fear and anxiety of losing ourselves. Celibacy without intimacy is a dead thing. Celibacy without warmth is lethal.

For persons in ministry, intimacy is not a choice. According to Erikson's stages of development, before persons in ministry can achieve the stage of generativity, (i.e., the stage at which the person, having received and accepted self, is able to reach out to give to others in creative and productive ways) they must be capable of intimacy.

In a community that has achieved a level of intimacy, members begin to think in terms of "we." Genuine friendship with others is the stepping-off point for growing in intimacy with God. The spirit of prayer, both individual and group, grows as persons share their feelings and thoughts, such as where God is leading them through the events of their daily lives. Nonaffirmed persons resisting intimacy often escape into workaholism. The apostolate can absorb their time so that they have nothing left to share in community. They become addicted to their apostolate, seeking affirmation where it can never be fully found.

To be in a relationship raises fear of being hurt; to be alone raises fear of losing self. Each of us experiences the drive toward intimacy, even as we experience the drive toward autonomy.

The drives of intimacy and autonomy create a tension that arouses both anger and affection. Our observations indicate that both emotions are extremely difficult for religious to deal with effectively, an observation supported by a study done on American priests by their bishops.[5] It noted that one of the main problems of clergy is their inability to be in touch with and accept their feelings and needs, especially their aggressive impulses. Though this study was of priests, we believe that the findings could apply equally to other persons in ministry.

Let's look at anger. Feelings of anger are generally expressed as a reaction to a diminution of our self-esteem or sense of worth. This diminishment may be real or imagined, but the reaction is the same. If our past has taught us to think of anger as wrong, then feeling angry may be perceived as being a bad religious. To avoid being bad, we believe we must avoid any situation that might produce anger. Since disagreement, conflict, and confrontation arouse anger, we believe we must avoid them. As a result, we miss many opportunities for growing and helping others to grow.

Attempts to deny feelings set up a process in which feelings (especially anger) go underground. The anger is turned in on ourselves or expressed in a destructive way. Anger turned inward may result in depression. In our work we see many religious and priests who are depressed. The unconscious logic runs like this: To be angry is bad. To be depressed is neither good nor bad. So, of the two, depression is the better.

Destructive anger may take the form of physical illness, e.g., migraine headaches, ulcers, or backaches. When we can view anger as a fact, a feeling, or an emotion, and emotions as neither good nor bad, we are in a better position to defuse anger's power over us.

Anger may be thought of as a fuse. Often we hear people say, "I blew a fuse." The emotion of anger is telling us something if we will listen. From experience, we know that overloading the system causes a short circuit; the fuse reacts to the overloading. The solution is to reduce the load. The same theory applies to anger. When we are in touch with our feelings of anger and we realize that anger is dominating our life, then we should search the system to find out where it is coming from. Most likely there is something wrong in our interpersonal relationships. If this is the source, we must analyze it and take steps to get the pressure reduced. This may entail confrontation. When we cannot express anger in a constructive fashion we may resort to hostility to communicate the hurt. Persons who are constantly expressing hostility are trying to tell us that they are hurting. Too often we focus on the anger and behavior and fail to hear the message of hurt. When this happens, the persons are reinforced in their feelings of anger over not being heard. It must be remembered that anger is always communicated. If we don't talk about it we act it out, and this can cause tension and even destruction in relationships.

Affection is a second element in intimacy. It may seem strange that this is also a difficult emotion for religious to handle. Affection is a natural consequence of living in a group. Sometimes religious appear to be more effective in dealing with anger than in dealing with affection, since more religious seem to be fighting than loving.

Some people are uncomfortable with feelings of affection. Our culture, especially our religious culture, may not have helped us to be comfortable with our own sexuality. This becomes evident in our fear of particular friendships and in regulations that were deterrents to the building of warm relationships. Today the fear of homosexuality may be an inhibiting factor. Much energy is expended by people in community trying to avoid normal feelings of anger and affection.

In the past we were discouraged from dealing with our feelings, particularly feelings evoked by intimacy. Now we are encouraging closeness and intimacy as necessary elements in becoming mature and fully human. This new perspective can result in even more tensions. And while we may have stopped recognizing our feelings, the emotions have not stopped stimulating the glands and thus potentially bringing on disease. Ignored emotions in the community account for the inability of some persons to risk vulnerability, getting involved, and investing in a new group. In addition, some persons assume that intimacy wipes out loneliness. But it must be recognized that no matter how close we feel to a group, we can and will still experience loneliness. Each of us needs the pain of loneliness to help us get in closer touch with ourselves and appreciate more fully the love of others. Intimacy is enhanced by our solitude.

When intimacy is a fact in community, those involved will be mature, not just psychologically sophisticated. We have invented a vocabulary for talking about personal intimacy, but the development of the skills needed for it seems to have lagged far behind. Philosopher Arthur Schopenhauer's famous simile of the freezing porcupines illustrates the ambivalence we usually experience in relationships: "A company of porcupines crowded themselves very close together one cold winter's day so as to profit by one another's warmth and so save themselves from being frozen to death. But soon they felt one another's quills, which induced them to separate again. And now, when the need for warmth brought them nearer again, the second evil arose once more. So they were driven backwards and forwards from one trouble to the other, until they had discovered a mean distance at which they could most tolerably exist."[6] It is a difficult task to discover how close or far we wish to become in community.

STAGE 8: TERMINATION

The final stage in all groups is termination. Termination is usually a difficult and painful experience for the members of the group, especially if they have progressed through the above stages. More and more of the current literature indicates that the greatest causes of stress in life are activities that produce termination, separation, and loss. Termination usually arouses in us a myriad of feelings, many of which are painful. It frequently recalls previous experiences of loss that have not been adequately dealt with or resolved. Terminations precipitate ambivalent feelings. An example of this is the experience of graduation, in which the graduates feel the sense of joy at having completed the years of schooling and look forward with hope and expectation to moving on to something new. This sense of joy, however, is coupled with intense feelings of sadness about leaving behind familiar persons, places, and situations. This feeling of finality can be all-pervasive.

Interesting dynamics are triggered by termination. The most general finding is that people try to avoid dealing with termination and the resultant feelings. However, these cannot be denied or avoided. People find it too hard to talk about them directly and more often refer to them in a symbolic way. The themes of death, sickness, and other losses are almost obsessive topics of people experiencing termination in groups. When termination is not talked about even symbolically, it will often be acted out in rather bizarre, regressive behavior. Some members will act as if they have never met before. Or they adopt the "I could care less" attitude. This is because it is easier to leave something you don't care about than it is to leave something you really cherish. Thus some people who come to the end of a relationship can handle this termination only by acting as if it had never existed.

Termination occurs whenever the group as it exists comes to an end. It might be that the group was formed for only a year and the year has ended, or a member of the group has died or left the group in the middle of the year. Whatever the cause, termination is often a traumatic experience for the persons involved, especially if the community experience has been a good one.

When we encourage closeness and intimacy in community living, we are putting people in a double bind. We promote the closeness but do not adequately prepare people for the pain of termination. When religious have invested themselves emotionally in a particular apostolate or with certain groups of people, termination can be likened to divorce, particularly when it involves change to a place geographically distant from where they have sunk roots. Only infrequently have religious communities acknowledged that termination might be difficult not just for those who are leaving but also for those who are left behind.

Often those who are left behind feel the greater pain, since those leaving feel an excitement mixed with the loss in going on to something new. But those left behind feel only the emptiness.

We must not only advert to the difficulty of termination but must also help people work through it and not insulate themselves from pain. Unless this is done, they will not be able to reinvest themselves emotionally in new situations. Failure to work through terminations causes serious emotional drains on people. As they become more aware of the dynamics of termination, some religious tend to discover ways of avoiding it altogether. We must look at how we can help people deal with termination more constructively so that it can be a source of growth in their lives. We must provide opportunities for people to talk about their feelings in advance of the actual termination. Time is required to work through all the levels of feelings. Evaluation of the group efforts for the year is helpful, if in the end, members can see what the group as a whole has achieved and what they personally have gained. The value of the group will remain in their memory for future reference. Even though every group ends, the things we as members have given and have received, the ways in which we have grown, and the skills we have learned all continue with us. It is important (1) that the group complete any unfinished business, (2) that the members relive and remember the positive group experiences they have had, (3) that the members integrate what they have received from being part of the group by reflecting and sharing, and (4) that members describe and express constructively their feelings about the termination of the group.

There is a need to ritualize all terminations; without it, grieving is incomplete. Often religious communities celebrate the end of the year but do not make it explicit that it is a way of ritualizing the end of the group. The greater the degree of group cohesiveness, the greater the need to talk about and celebrate the termination.

Ultimately, we must bring our own Christian values to the experience of termination. We claim to be Death-Resurrection people. This is what our life is all about. We do not want to avoid death. Instead, through death we discover a greater fullness of the mystery of the Resurrection. Where there is no experience of death and resurrection, community life is unreal. To live in community is to experience a rhythm of light and darkness, faith and doubt, and love and loneliness.

Whenever a new member comes to or leaves the community a new group is formed. This precipitates new patterns of interaction. The same is true when the end of the year comes and various members are dispersed for a period of time or undergo new experiences unrelated to the local group; there will be changes in patterns of interaction. Since members have been exposed to experiences that have resulted in some growth and change, when they return to the group they are different from when they left. Changes in interaction patterns may also result from a traumatic event or some experience that deeply touches the lives of all the members. (For further discussion of this subject, see Appendix.)

CONCLUSION

Our hope is that in reading this chapter you have recognized some of the ordinary community dynamics you have experienced. Are you able to look realistically at where your community is and accept it so that you may begin to look at where it might go? As a member of the community, can you begin to see how you can help it proceed to the next stage of its development?

Knowing the stages through which a group progresses is only the first step. Taking the risks involved to move it to the next stage is the second. Communities need to talk about what's happening and raise to a conscious level the dynamics of their living together. Then they can look at the dynamics honestly and create a climate in which they to share faith and live at a more human level.

In other chapters we will focus on communication in community and explore the dynamics that facilitate or hinder our ability to communicate with one another in a caring way. Keep in mind that stages of group growth are cyclic. Each time the group changes, each time a new year begins, each time a new member is added or one leaves, the process begins again, and a new group is formed.

NOTES

1. Erik Erikson, *Childhood and Society* (New York: Norton and Co., 1963), pp. 247–274.
2. Sigmund Freud, *Group Psychology and the Analysis of the Ego* (New York: Bantam Books, 1960), p. 95.
3. Irving Yalom, *The Theory and Prac-*

tice of Group Psychotherapy (New York: Basic Books, 1970), p. 91.

4. *Ibid*, p. 53.

5. National Opinion Research Center, *The Catholic Priest in the United States: Sociological Investigations* (Washington, D.C.: United States Catholic Conference, 1972), p. 68.

6. Arthur Schopenhauer, *Parerga und Paralipomena* (London: Allen and Univin, 1951), part 2, 31.

III

Group Dynamics

Some groups seem to grow, make progress, and remain healthy, while others seem to stagnate, go nowhere, and appear sick. We believe that understanding the dynamics of groups can influence the direction of a community and also contribute to the growth of its individual members.

In this chapter, we will present some aspects of group dynamics based on reported studies of groups. These findings will be supplemented by our experiences with and observations of religious communities we have worked with.

INDIVIDUAL BEHAVIOR IN GROUP MOTIVATED BY PERSONAL NEEDS

Behavior is initially learned through interaction with our parents and siblings. These behavior patterns are continued in later relationships. Unconsciously, we attempt to meet our needs in later groups in the same way they were met in the original nuclear family. Whatever served to get attention in the family group is continued. Members of a community often see the community through the glasses of their experiences and needs, and not as it really is. This causes frustration among group members and interferes with communication. Most of this distortion is unconscious, which adds to the confusion and frustration. One community member is ingratiating, another submissive, and yet another aggressive. Each is recreating his original family relationship. How the child acted when frustrated by the family group is now transferred; a similar response is made to the frustration in the current group. However, the response of the six-year-old child is no longer appropriate. People can change early learned patterns of response and reaction to more appropriate ones once they are aware of them.

GROUP DEFENSES

Just as individuals employ defenses to protect their self-esteem when they are threatened, so does a group react when it experiences threat. Such reactions are called group defenses and operate to protect the members from dealing with potential feelings of inadequacy, insecurity, or loss of self-esteem. Some defenses are used by individuals and groups, and some are specifically group defenses. We will describe five of them: dependency, pairing, fight or flight, scapegoating, and splitting. Remember, defenses are unconscious, the group is unaware of what it is doing and why.

Dependency. When a group feels threatened, it may react by behaving as if it is incapable of doing anything on its own. Looking in on a group employing this defense, we would assume that the entire group consists of people absolutely dependent on someone or something else for their safety and security.

Consider a meeting of a group of sisters. They have reached a point at which conflict seems imminent. But the group fears conflict. As a result, it begins to act as though it is incapable of handling even the simplest task on the agenda. Sometimes one person in the group rushes in to rescue these poor, incompetent, dependent people. The only problem is that the members really do not want to be rescued because then they will be forced to face the conflict. Dependency is a defense against this frightening encounter. The person who has rushed in to rescue the group will receive the same reward our Savior did—crucifixion. The unconscious theme of the group is, "Kill the Rescuer! We don't want to face reality." Whenever this appears to be happening, we recommend forcing the group to step back and explore what may be impelling them to attempt such a form of resistance.

If there is a designated leader in the group, this person will begin to feel weighed down by the group's dependency. Nothing seems to move them beyond this state. Once the group is forced to look at the cause of its reaction, it will be able to let go of the dependency.

Sometimes the group looks for salvation outside itself to avoid conflict—it acts as though it is completely dependent on a document, such as the constitution or latest directive from the general council, which will provide the answers to all problems. It clings to this for protection against the impending, unavoidable conflict. When confronted with this type of resistance, some member needs to challenge the group to recognize its resistance, look at its cause, and try to defuse the fear underlying it.

Pairing. Another form of defense is pairing. It can be of two types, positive and negative. Positive pairing occurs when the group allows two of the members to do all the talking in the group. The two get into dialogue with each other while the rest of the group sit idly by as interested or passive spectators. This frees the group as a whole from taking responsibility by placing it all in the hands of two group members.

A community of brothers at a house meeting are discussing the difficult issue of intimacy and how they deal with it in their own lives. Gradually, as the discussion becomes threatening, the majority of the members retreat to the sidelines and become passive observers. Two of the more articulate members carry on the dialogue. The rest listen and watch but remain in safe, secure, nonparticipatory, nonrevealing roles. All attention becomes riveted on the two actors while silent members root for them to come up with magical answers to solve the tension. The group abdicates its responsibility to grapple with the issue while it manipulates two members into doing all its work.

Pairing is a response to a threat. To move the group beyond

this threat someone has to have the insight and courage to gently challenge all members of the group to share their feelings, thoughts, and reactions to the issue at hand.

Negative pairing reflects a tendency toward polarization. As in positive pairing, two people, or two sides, take divergent points of view. A debate develops with proponents of each viewpoint taking strong positions. Pairing is said to occur if the majority of members take a passive role, leaving two articulate members to do battle. It is similar to a tennis match in which two opponents hit a ball back and forth across the net, while the people in the stands continue to follow the process. They are interested but don't get actively involved in the action.

One sister who found herself in this position described it to us graphically. "Once I declared where I stood on the subject, I found myself taking a more extreme point of view each time I was challenged by the sister who had stated the opposite point of view. By the end of the meeting, the argument had escalated to the point where I was defending positions that I didn't really believe. Meanwhile, the rest of the community simply observed and remained silent. The two of us seemed to be setting the extreme positions on a continuum of beliefs, while community members sat by safely and undeclared as to where along the continuum they stood. When it was over, I felt like a complete fool. I felt I'd been manipulated."

When this sort of negative pairing begins, others in the group can assume responsibility and courageously interrupt. This gives the two involved people distance and challenges the others to indicate their stance. It is even more important to get members to give reasons for what they believe. Pairing is a group defense to resist commitment. When one pairing defense is blocked it is important to be firm in not allowing it to develop with two other people. Take time to pray or reflect when needed. Set ground rules that can assist people in listening to one another without resorting immediately to defensiveness.

Fight or Flight. Fight or flight is another defense assumed by the group to resist dealing with difficult material. The fighting may be intragroup, but more frequently the group will band together to do battle with a common enemy outside the community. This outside enemy is labeled as the real cause of whatever problems exist in the community. Persons in administration make excellent targets.

Fear or resistance can also be dealt with through the many forms of flight. The group may simply decide to be silent or to talk about another topic that is nonthreatening. It can also conveniently discover reasons for postponing or eliminating meetings. A number of examples of this defense have been given in other sections of this book.

Scapegoating. Scapegoating is probably the most destructive of all the group defenses. It is a term which has its roots in the Old Testament. The early Israelites atoned for their sins by selecting a goat or other animal, either destroying it or driving it out into the desert. This act symbolically represented the removal of sins.

Scapegoating is the modern version of this expiation. When there is something within us we find distasteful, we can deny its existence in ourselves and project it onto a victim. We destroy or drive our victim away, in the unconscious hope of removing what is unacceptable about ourselves.

In communities, scapegoating can take many forms. In some cases we attempt to find someone to blame for all our problems: "If only Sister X weren't here, everything would be all right." In the past, alcoholics made great scapegoats in communities: "We really can't have any community meetings because you know how Father Y reacts when he's been drinking." Sometimes the scapegoated person is not even living in the community: "If that Provincial would only do this and that, everything would be great." It reaches its most extreme forms when the scapegoat is an inanimate object. In many communities cars, keys, and money are blamed for everything. When you witness a community in which great emotion is aroused over inanimate objects, the liturgy, community prayers, etc., the emotion is probably being displaced onto the wrong object or issue. As a rule of thumb, whenever there is an inordinate amount of emotion or energy being expended on superficial topics, the issue is really persons and personalities. We project anger onto objects because we are more comfortable dealing with them than with persons.

The greatest problem with the use of scapegoating is that it doesn't change anything. As long as blame can be projected onto another person or thing there is no force or need for self-confrontation and change. A study done with the families of schizophrenic children sheds some light on this. The researchers discovered that when one schizophrenic child in a family was cured, another child in the family would often become schizophrenic. It was as though that family system needed a sick child to function. The question for us in communities to answer is whether we also need to label some people as sick or problematic and to blame them for all that is wrong. Does doing so free us from the difficult task of looking at our own inadequacies and failings?

One of the interesting aspects of scapegoating is that the scapegoated person permits it. Scapegoating usually flourishes on half truths. We identify someone, for instance, who has a quick temper. The entire community subtly reaches an agreement that the problem in this house is the tension caused by Brother R's emotional outbursts. It follows that if the group could eliminate Brother R, everything would be perfect. If Brother R accepts this blame, it frees the rest of the community from looking at other sources or causes of tension within the house. Ultimately the community, like the penitent of old, will attempt to drive this scapegoat out of the house. Should Brother R leave, someone else will replace him; the group needs a scapegoat.

One of the more subtle forms of scapegoating involves identifying the obsessive talkers. Whenever the meeting becomes too threatening, the group unconsciously encourages these persons to "do their thing." As they go on incessantly, the community is able to blame them for the inability to have effective meetings: "If only they would shut up, we could get something done." They fail to recognize that one or two individuals cannot dominate a meeting unless the others allow it. Whenever we give one member of a group that much power, the problem is the passivity of the majority.

As we mentioned earlier, scapegoating is destructive. Any time we become aware of it, we must act immediately to stop it. One way of doing this is to point out to the group that all of us need to change. Changing or removing one person is not the solution. We can initiate this by sharing what we personally can do to alleviate the situation and by encouraging others to do the same.

Splitting. One of the more interesting group defenses is splitting. Splitting is a dynamic that operates especially when there are two leaders for the group. The group attributes all goodness to one leader and all badness to the other. It is a complete dichotomy.

Since regression often takes place in a group and the members revert to childhood roles and behavior, splitting may be a repetition of a childhood attempt to split the parents and cause polarization between them.

We had the experience of working with two different groups of women religious in which this occurred. In one group, every "smart" intervention was credited to the male leader, regardless of which of us had made the intervention. Significantly, this was a group in which the women had a low sense of self-esteem. The experience had a predictable effect on us as leaders. The man came out feeling superior and good about himself. The woman, on the other hand, felt hurt and angry. The group had been effective in accomplishing what they desired. Once we were able to dialogue about it, we could see more clearly what had been occurring. This understanding enabled us to avoid getting caught again in the defense the group was using to resist dealing with difficult issues.

In the other group, which consisted of women growing in their sense of self-esteem, the roles were reversed. The female leader was seen as all wise and all good and the man was seen as being an inept obstructionist.

When a group does not have facilitators, it may attempt to split two of the more powerful members.

UNREALISTIC EXPECTATIONS

All of us have unarticulated ideas about what we expect of others and what others expect of us. These ideas are seldom shared.

One of the problems in community life today is that many

people have very unrealistic expectations of community. Unrealistic expectations cause frustration, and we all have our characteristic method for coping with it. Most frequently it is the fight or flight response.

Some people expect community to meet their needs just as satisfactorily as they were met in intimate family life. But community is not a family, was never intended to be a family, and is incapable of meeting many needs often met fully in a family. The problem has been compounded by the many articles that paint an unrealistic, idealistic picture of what community life can and should be. In addition, early formation programs have often reinforced this idealistic picture. People whose expectations are unrealistic are going to experience a great amount of frustration and dissatisfaction with community. Rather than realistically and maturely reassessing and readjusting them, these people will go through life angry and resentful because the community failed to meet their unattainable expectations.

One of the fears we have in presenting this book is that unintentionally we may reinforce a reader's unrealistic image of what community should be. We remind our readers again that community is a process, always ongoing and incomplete. Perfect community is never achieved but rather exists as an ideal toward which we are always moving.

CONDITIONS THAT ENGENDER GROWTH, HEALING, AND CHANGE IN GROUPS

Although most of the better research on groups has been conducted with therapy groups, the findings have relevance for all groups, including community. What are the conditions necessary for the growth of a group? Since each of us belongs to more than one group, it is important to know these conditions.

Every healthy group is therapeutic; i.e., every healthy group assists its members to grow. We want to emphasize that we are using the term therapeutic in the context of facilitating growth. It is not synonymous with therapy. Community groups should be therapeutic, inasmuch as they assist members to grow to the fullness of their life in Christ. They are not therapy groups since

CONDITIONS THAT ENGENDER GROWTH, HEALING, AND CHANGE IN GROUPS

Members begin with a commitment to discuss problems openly, to change behavior, and to help others change their behavior.

Before they begin members know what is expected of them, insofar as this is possible.

Members accept responsibility for helping to develop and maintain a therapeutic climate.

Members sense genuine acceptance within their group.

Members perceive their group as attractive.

Members feel they truly belong.

Members feel safe enough within the group to discuss whatever bothers them.

Members experience enough tension to want to change, believe that they can cope with their tension, and are convinced that the results will be worth the pain and effort.

Members accept the group's norms.

intrapsychic changes in the personalities of each member are not the primary purpose.

Group theorist Merle Ohlsen has listed nine conditions that he believes must be present if a group is to achieve its potential for growth, healing, and change.[1]

1. Members begin with a commitment to discuss problems openly, to change behavior, and to help others change their behavior.
2. Members know, before they begin, what is expected of them, insofar as this is possible.
3. Members accept responsibility for helping to develop and maintain a therapeutic climate.
4. Members sense genuine acceptance within their group.
5. Members perceive their group as attractive.
6. Members feel they truly belong.
7. Members feel safe enough within the group to discuss whatever bothers them.
8. Members experience enough tension to want to change, believe they can cope with their tension, and are convinced the results will be worth the pain and effort.
9. Members accept the group's norms.

Let's look at each of these conditions separately to see what they mean for religious communities.

1. *Members begin with a commitment to discuss problems openly, to change behavior, and to help others change their behavior.* When we are called to community, we come with the expectation that we can be open in sharing ourselves and receiving from others the help that we need to grow. The more aware we become of our weaknesses, immaturities, and inner poverties the harder we find it to face them. It is much easier to criticize others for the faults we cannot face in ourselves.

If there is to be a willingness to discuss openly the issues causing problems in the growth of the community, members need to come to the community with the conviction that there are areas in which they must grow personally, spiritually, and apostolicly. This conviction must be accompanied by a belief that the community will assist them in identifying areas of needed growth, which, however, is possible only if they are willing to articulate their needs and problems.

We often blame the community and its members for not being

responsive to our needs when the real problem is that we have not articulated them. If persons living together expect the other members to be mind readers, their lives together are likely to be unrewarding and frustrating. Others generally cannot know our good intentions and needs without being told. When members are left uninformed and remain unresponsive, anger will character- ize the group, but no one will be able to point out its source.

We assume that all members of the community come to it fully aware that change is a constant in the life process. We are always being called by the Lord to new and different ways of growing in the fullness of His life in us, of revealing His giftedness in us. Change is an everyday and necessary part of our lives, yet resistance to change seems to be one of the greatest problems in community life. We all resist personal change. Our commitment to community implies a dependence and an interdependence that is an affront to our basic need for independence, and we live with fear that community life is robbing us of our individuality. If our community life is to be growth producing, we must be open to frequent and at times dramatic change. Change, another word for growth, must always have direction and purpose. These are dis- covered through personal discernment. We rely on friends and other sources of support to help us determine what changes we need to make in response to the Spirit working within us. Not to change is to refuse to grow, and this is death.

Psychiatrist Angelo D'Agostino, S.J., speaking at Holy Trinity Seminary in Silver Spring, Maryland, remarked that the pre–Vat- ican II Church encouraged people's tendency to be obsessive- compulsive. The good religious of pre–Vatican II days were those who were predictably consistent. They kept the same schedule every day of their religious lives. They repeated the same prayers at the same time and in the same manner every day. This was the usual criterion on which we based our judgment of the good reli- gious. In the post–Vatican II Church, D'Agostino pointed out, the position is reversed. Good religious are those who are flexible and adaptable. They are no longer those who are rigid in adhering to constancy but rather those who can meet the constantly changing realities of life around them.

People in community must be willing to help and support other members in making whatever changes are necessary for that individual and/or the community. This support demands personal involvement in the lives of other members of our communities; it requires a willingness to take the time and to invest ourselves in getting to know those we live with. It is easier and more comfortable to settle for knowing only basic facts about another person—name, rank, and serial number—while respecting the corresponding impersonal "Do not fold, spindle, or mutilate." We may know something about what others in the group do and where they come from but little about their dreams, hopes, or fears. We cannot assist others in the change process unless we know them more intimately. If we appear to expect too much of persons and refuse to allow them to be themselves, we cannot realistically hope they will be ready to take the risks involved in trust and self-disclosure, two essentials necessary if change is to occur. We can accept the suggestions and advice of others only when we feel they sincerely care about us and accept us with genuine understanding. If we suspect others of trying to help us only to meet their own needs or sense of duty, we will quickly reject their assistance.

Many of our observations are supported by psychiatrists and psychologists who have undertaken research on groups. In studying groups, Jerome Frank discovered that the most effective were those that allowed free and honest expression of feelings and in which members had the opportunity to discuss their own and others' problems constructively.[3] He concluded that free discussion also diminished the feelings of isolation and increased the members' sense of hope and self-esteem.

The implication of Frank's study for religious communities is that when we create a milieu in which people feel free to discuss problems openly, the members will experience greater self-esteem and a greater sense of Christian hope.

Rudolph Dreikurs found that the spirit of openness in a group is dependent on the members' feelings of belonging.[3] Members must experience a genuine fellowship, in which persons give of themselves without ulterior motives.

A climate for open discussion requires that members of the community feel they are really important. Ohlsen suggests that a group that provides this accepting climate makes it possible for a person not only to learn from the group experience but also to transfer what is learned to situations encountered in daily life.[4] By experiencing a group climate in which others are willing to help analyze failures and rejoice in successes, a person can risk similar behavior in daily living. Unfortunately, many of our communities are not places where sharing daily experiences is encouraged, especially the ones that entail an emotional response.

2. *Members know, before they begin, what is expected of them, insofar as this is possible.* Expectations play an important role in communities. We have stated elsewhere that unrealistic expectations lead to much of the frustration encountered in community living. Since it is a prevalent problem, a community would benefit from taking time early in its life for members to explore and clarify expectations of one another at both the communal and the personal level. Ohlsen believes that the ideal time to explore expectations is before the person gets to community.[5] New members are often still dealing with the termination and loss involved in leaving previous apostolates and residences at the same time they are coming to grips with their new situation and needs for inclusion. The transition is especially painful for the person who has experienced a caring group in the previous assignment. Any way in which the community can assist new members in making a smooth transition should be applied.

While the person entering the community brings expectations, the community receiving the person also has a set of expectations for its members. These are usually limited to the minimum of what is necessary for efficient and productive functioning of the community, such as general house maintenance, communal prayer, and house meetings. Another set of expectations may set the maximum ideal of the group, or the ideal of the perfect community. These expectations would deal with the ways the community has chosen to manage tension.

Discussion and negotiation of both minimum expectations and maximum ideals is a mutual responsibility of the new member and the community group. Unfortunately, many communities continue to live by the expectations set up in previous years by members long departed. Each time a group either receives or loses a member, it becomes a new group. Group expectations should be reviewed, negotiated, and agreed upon by this new group. If the existing community and new members moving into it cannot agree on norms, the new members would do well to reconsider their decision to join this community.

We know of one community in which much time was spent developing expectations of one another and of the community. Expectations were so clearly articulated and lived that new persons coming into the group were well aware of what was expected of them as they joined the group and were able to evaluate and decide whether this was a good community for them. This group is currently a very effective community.

One person who went through the process of determining her commitment to this community recently shared with us the fears she experienced before engaging in the process. She also expressed the great satisfaction and peace that followed her decision. Her fears were derived from her feelings that this community was an elite group that was judging and evaluating her. Her experience was just the opposite. She discovered that she was being asked to enter into a communal life in which she and the other members must struggle mutually to grow together. She realized that the other community members were there not to judge her but to support her while they experienced the same things. She discovered that this was the basis for their growth in communal life. She felt that for the first time in her life she was entering a community experience with a sense of clarity of her expectations and of the expectations of others. Although she has since moved to another community, the positive values learned through this experience have had a lasting influence on her and her attitude toward community.

3. *Members accept responsibility for helping to develop and maintain a therapeutic climate.* In their research Charles B. Truax and Robert R. Carkhuff found that effective therapists established warm, accepting, understanding relationships with their patients.[6] We believe that for any group to be effective the same relationship must exist among members. A climate conducive to helping people feel free to share what they think and feel must be established. Our experience has been that no group proceeds beyond an initial stage until a supportive climate exists. While the research of Traux and Carkhuff places this responsibility on the therapist, we believe that the responsibility rests on every member of the community. Only through the efforts of each member

can the community move to a climate characterized by warmth, acceptance, understanding, and freedom. Unless this occurs, the members of the community will remain in positions of mutual defensiveness, more concerned about proving their adequacy and protecting themselves than in being present for the others. These defenses deplete the energy that could be used to function as a community growing together toward the freedom of God.

One of the primary ways of establishing this climate is to develop the ability to listen to one another. Listening is a rare skill. Too often we concentrate on what another person is saying and never hear the feeling behind the words, the real message. This situation takes us back to the mind reading that goes on in community. We don't listen because we assume that we already know what this person thinks and feels even before they are described. We leave community meetings or sharing sessions and are amazed later to discover the numerous interpretations of what happened or what was said there.

The following example illustrates this point. Sister A has come into conflict with her community over the issue of community prayer. She is intensely in favor of spontaneous community prayer, while the group prefers the Prayer of Christians. The community does not comprehend the reason for the intensity of her desire. Much of the emotional outburst is probably related to the fact that Sister A feels that no one understands her. The issue of prayer is incidental. The community could be more helpful if it would allow or encourage Sister A to explore her strong feelings. Persons who feel understood can lower their defenses and consequently be more open to listening to the other side of the issue. When uninvolved community members take responsibility for helping those emotionally involved to get to the *why* behind the *what*, a healthier climate is established in the community.

The difficulty in listening is well described by John Powell: "To understand people, I must try to hear what they are *not* saying, what they perhaps will never be able to say."[7] Another sensitive description of the difficulty of listening is found in Marjorie Kellogg's story, *Tell Me that You Love Me Junie Moon*. In the novel we are introduced to three young adults, each of whom suffers from a physical disability. They have learned to cope with their disability by being somewhat cynical. At one point Junie decides to work on creating a warmer climate in the group by making a gentle remark. One of the young men, Arthur, responds in his usual caustic way. Junie, in her frustration, declares:

> The trouble, Arthur, with you is that you seldom listen to me, and when you do you don't hear, and when you do hear you hear wrong, and even when you hear right you change it so fast that it's never the same.[8]

This quotation may describe our own experiences in community. We cannot share ourselves unless we feel that we are listened to, heard, and understood by a group of warm, concerned persons. Community takes time, but it is built on the small everyday gestures that allow persons to feel accepted without placing expectations on them that force them into playing a role for self-protection.

We often suffer in community from the elephant like memories of others. Things that were said or done 20 years ago when we were still in formation are still remembered, sticking to us like burrs. Most of us have been victims of this "unforgetting." Even when great growth has taken place in us, images or impressions stored in the memory bank of others are pulled out to color and distort their perception of our motivations and attitudes. The resulting frustration and lack of forgiveness of memories constitute a block to establishing the desired climate. Our chapter on communication will indicate many ways in which the caring climate can be developed.

4. *Members sense a genuine acceptance within their group.* One of the classic works in group research has been conducted by Irving Yalom. He emphasizes that each member of the group has to feel acceptance.

> Universality and catharsis, for example, are part processes. It is not the sheer process of ventilation that is important, it is not only the discovery of others' disconfirmation of our wretched uniqueness that is important; it is the affective sharing of one's inner world and *then* acceptance by others that seems of paramount importance. Being accepted by others despite one's fantasies of being basically repugnant, unacceptable, or unlovable is a potent healing force.[9]

In studying patients who stated they were improved or who expressed regret at leaving the group prematurely, Yalom discovered three basic similarities: (1) they felt accepted by the other members; (2) they perceived a similarity of some kind among group members; and (3) when queried about their group experience, they made specific references to particular individuals.[10] In both situations, Yalom points out the absolute need for people to feel accepted if the group or community experience is to be growth producing. In a similar vein, W. J. Sprott has concluded that "it is only through the approval of others that the self can tolerate the self."[11]

It becomes imperative then that persons living in community begin to assess the degree to which they are communicating a real sense of acceptance to one another. Do we really accept others with their weaknesses, immaturities, and flaws, or has religious life conditioned us to the point that we expect nothing short of perfection in ourselves and in others? Our own failings are not easy for us to accept, and as a defense we develop a perfectionistic attitude toward others. We refuse to accept them as they are and project an attitude of nonacceptance. It is only when we are able to accept ourselves with our shadows, darknesses, and immaturities that we will be able to reach out and accept the same weaknesses and faults in others. When we can accept God's forgiveness of ourselves, then we can accept and forgive others. We can begin to take a more Christian attitude based on the belief that each member of the community, made in the image and likeness of God, is gifted and called by God to play a very definite role in continuing the work and mission of Jesus in the world. As we are able to see one another through these attitudes, our feelings of mutual acceptance and love for persons go beyond acceptance based merely on personal attraction.

There is a cliche that says we need to accept persons even when we reject their behavior. This is more than a truism. Some behavior is self-destructive or other-destructive. Are we able to see the goodness of the people we live with, accepting them with a real sense of love and concern, yet confronting them when their behavior is either self-destructive or other-destructive?

This approach has been used effectively in dealing with alcoholics in community. The alcoholic is engaging in self-destructive behavior. When members of the community can convey their respect and concern for the alcoholic even while pointing out their nonacceptance of the destructive behavior, the person can often accept the confrontation that would otherwise be ineffective. Under these circumstances, confronting behavior can be synonymous with communicating basic acceptance.

We all need to experience acceptance. Reflect for a moment on an experience you have had in which you felt truly accepted by another. Who was the person? How did their acceptance free you to be yourself and to let down your defenses? What does it say to you about what you can do for others in the community? How can you communicate your acceptance to them?

5. *Members perceive their group as attractive.* According to research conducted by Dorwin Cartwright, some of the conditions that make a group attractive are (1) group members are valued and accepted; (2) the group provides opportunities for social life and close personal association; and (3) the group provides at least two of the following three sources of satisfaction: personal attraction, task attraction, or prestige from membership.[12]

These three conditions provide a background for looking at a number of issues. First, members must feel valued and accepted if the group is to be seen as attractive. We have already discussed the concept of acceptance. What about being valued? Who are the people in our communities who are most valued? Living in a society that is greatly influenced by the work ethic and the competitive system, we have often unconsciously absorbed the same values within religious communities. In subtle ways we place a priority on productivity and prestige. We are more concerned about what a person does than about who that person is. We operate in a double bind when we state that who we are is the real priority, but we develop a system of rewards based on productivity or on what we do. It has been a personal sorrow to us as we have worked with communities to listen to older members discussing their anticipated or present retirement. Many express outright their feelings of pain. Since they can no longer produce, they feel valueless and a drain on community. This has become more prevalent today as communities attract fewer vocations and are adversely affected by our inflationary economy. Greater emphasis is directed toward community finances and this often places subtle pressure on community members to choose apostolates and ministries that will provide needed income. Those no longer able to contribute monetarily suffer from a sense of burden they believe they place on their community. These older religious equate their value with their productivity. This attitude should be of great concern to a community. Every community needs to assess the prevalence of this attitude and the community structures that contribute to the sense of devaluation experienced by nonearning members.

One source of communicating values within a community is the community newsletter. With what and with whom are newsletters concerned? Who are the persons who receive the most coverage? Our observations indicate that they are usually persons who have apostolates and ministries that are most dramatic, different, and sensational. Persons in the more traditional ministries detect that what they are doing is not being valued since it is ignored. How much newsletter coverage is given to people no longer able to engage in active and productive ministries? As these persons grow older, their names are rarely noted unless they are doing something newsworthy or unusual, thus there is little reason for them to feel that they are still valued.

Recently, we met a navy chaplain who was wearing various ribbons and medals on the front of his jacket. Proudly he explained the meaning of the different awards and then sadly compared his experience in the service with his experience in his community. He had been in charge of formation in his community for five years when he left this position to enter the chaplain corps. There was not so much as a cocktail party before the regular community meal to express appreciation for his years of service. He contrasted the military service and its tangible appreciation with experience in community where his contributions were taken for granted. This conversation convinced us further of the need for religious communities to recognize the personal value of members and to reinforce this through some expression of appreciation.

Reward systems in religious life are extremely limited. Few tangible, explicit rewards are given for being a good religious, for the quality of a religious life. Ministries take precedence. Our early training stressed service of the Lord as its own reward. Affirmation was considered unnecessary. Today, people's need to experience affirmation if they are to grow is an accepted concept.

We need some kind of yardstick to assure us that we are going in the right direction. As communities we must ask ourselves questions such as: What are the things we value in our members? How do we reinforce these values? Have we become victims of the society around us rather than a countersign to its values of over-productivity and wealth? What methods of reward and affirmation do we have for those who lead a good religious life? How sensitive are we to those who are no longer capable of active ministry? Are we overemphasizing the more dramatic ministries at the expense of the less dramatic?

To be attractive to its members, a group must satisfy the need for a social life and close personal relationships. On one occasion, when we were conducting a community group, we were overwhelmed by the intensity and seriousness of the group and so asked the question, "Do you believe that community should be fun?" From the incredulous looks we received, it was evident that this possibility had never been considered. Our question didn't even seem relevant to the group. This group was at a stage termed "survival." For survival communities, community life is something to be endured. We believe that God has called us to more than this. He has brought us together to help one another grow. We are not perfect communities. Struggle and tension will always be a part of our lives, but joy can exist alongside them. A community that doesn't play together loses one dimension of its life. After attending many community meetings with different groups, we have gotten the impression that some communities come together only to argue and fight—sometimes to pray. There is seldom a sense of coming together just for the purpose of socializing and enjoying one another's company. Communities seem extremely task oriented or problem centered. Coming together for sheer joy and fun is a low priority; this does not make community a very attractive option. How often does your local community come together just so people can enjoy one another?

We are not advocating that communities become places where all needs for social life and personal relationships are met. That is the closed system concept, in which the person relies on one system to meet all needs. This kind of system was encouraged in the past; it was even put forward as the ideal. But the closed system can be disastrous. When a person is dependent on one system for fulfillment of all needs, a situation is created in which it becomes impossible to deal with the confrontation and conflict essential for the growth of the community. To challenge the very system one is dependent on is extremely threatening. To be rejected by this system is to experience total rejection, and the risk is too great.

We are not suggesting that no needs be met in community. In the healthy community some needs are met within and some from outside. For example, we may meet spiritual and affiliation needs through persons in the community, yet have other needs met by friends and prayer groups that are external.

Another condition for group attractiveness is that the group provides satisfaction in at least two of three areas: personal attraction, task attraction, or prestige of membership. Reflect on your own community. What was your reason for choosing this particular congregation, society, or community? Was it the people, the apostolate, the reputation of the group, or something else? Was it the community spirit? What made this particular congregation attractive to you initially, and why have you continued to remain in it?

It is our belief that future communities will allow for greater pluralism and that expectations of new members will be more clearly articulated. Some communities will offer a more highly structured life-style; others will offer the opposite. Some groups will articulate broad ministries; others will remain specific. Choices, however, will be made on the basis of clearly stated expectations. While it can be anticipated that members would desire to belong to a group with a good reputation, we hope that prestige of membership would not be a major criterion.

6. *Members feel they truly belong.* Researchers Dorothy Beck and Herbert Kelman have explored the elements contributing to a sense of belonging. Beck found that a struggle shared with others contributed to it.[13] Kelman noted that the feeling of belonging was bolstered by discussions of intimate topics as well as by the support the group members provided for one another.[14]

Our sense of belonging is related to our experience of universality with others. It is enhanced when we experience ourselves as a group of committed Christians struggling together to discover the Lord's constantly evolving will. On occasion we may think we are alone in our spiritual, psychological, or emotional growth problems. We may feel a sense of isolation from the community. When we can share the struggle with one another, we can grasp the real potential for personal and communal growth.

Kelman's research indicates that intimacy is a prerequisite to feelings of belonging. As dreams, hopes, joys, sorrows, fears, and anxieties are shared with others in community, members experience a sense of being home, of being welcomed and cared for.

The importance of belonging was demonstrated to us when we were giving a one-week sexuality workshop for a large group. Those attending the workshop were all members of one congregation and the staff was a group of persons very competent in the topics selected. The day was divided between input by the experts and sessions for small-group sharing. The groups stayed together for the entire week. At the end, when evaluations were made of all aspects of the workshop, it became evident that while the talks were appreciated, the most important part of the week for the participants had been the sharing that took place in the small groups. These groups had developed to the point that members were able to communicate on an intimate level. It was not a show-and-tell or sensitivity session, but rather a sharing of struggles with their own humanness. In each small group people had felt a sense of acceptance and support. There were also ongoing results. In follow-up with the communities in attendance at that workshop we have found a definite and impressive growth in their ability to continue as supportive faith communities. Evaluations by the workshop participants confirmed Yalom's finding that most group members indicate that the primary mode of help in the group is mutual support.[15]

7. *Members feel safe enough within the group to discuss whatever bothers them.* Kelman suggests that we can benefit from group experience only if we are willing to make a commitment to the group situation.[16] Such a commitment is contingent on our belief that we will be safe and protected. In short, we must feel secure in the group before we are willing to discuss the issues that need to be explored. Without this open discussion the group experience is of little benefit to either the group or the individual.

In his theory of human development, Erikson proposes that the initial stage of all development is trust, as opposed to distrust.[17] No growth can take place until one person is able to trust another. What holds true for the development of the person is also true for the development of groups. In the group no progress can be made until all members believe that difficult but necessary issues can be discussed and that other members of the group can be trusted in such a discussion.

A group of persons who lived in different communities were reflecting on the fact that they could be so free in sharing with one another, but that such sharing was virtually impossible in their own local community setting. When pushed to explore the underlying reason for this, they reluctantly revealed that there was a lack of trust in the people they were living with. They did not feel safe enough to take a risk.

Most people have enough basic faith to trust others until there has been an experience to make them question that trust. Most of us entering a situation test others by sharing some bits of information. We then wait to see how others will respond or react. Gradually we ascertain the level at which we can trust them. This testing process, a gradual peeling away of defenses, is characteristic of the way we develop relationships. It allows us to share more of ourselves with others as we discover that trust is respected. Confident of this, we feel that the group is a safe place in which to explore relationships and learn more about ourselves and the situations that we face in the community.

We feel safe when we believe we will not be hurt even if our sharing is threatening to the group. As members of communities, we must be constantly sensitive to those moments when other members feel attacked or fearful of raising questions and issues important to them and to the group. We must pick up signals of defensiveness in our community discussions, such as attacks on others, and we must take the initiative to boldly suggest time out for privately reflecting on what is making us feel defensive. After looking for the cause, we must evaluate our own behavior and attitudes to see if we are responsible for the climate undermining the sense of safety.

Nothing can be more destructive to the feeling of safety in the group than the use of scapegoating to deal with difficult issues. If scapegoating is used on others, we know there is the probability that it will also be used on us. When scapegoating is observed, it is best to relate calmly our observation to the group, along with the suggestion that we all examine ways in which we might be contributing to the problem. The objective is to divert attention away from the scapegoat and toward the other members. When someone in the group takes this initiative, the climate of safety will grow and other members of the group will be more willing to risk themselves.

8. *Members experience enough tension to want to change, believe they can cope with their tension, and are convinced the results will be worth the pain and effort.* Somehow a myth has developed that the best of all human conditions is to be tension free. For many people a stress-free existence is the goal of life. And in our culture, for some it has become an obsession. During the last decade some excellent research was done on tension and stress. Periodicals, both secular and religious, are replete with articles on stress, tension, and burnout. Problems have arisen when persons reading the research have made naive interpretations, focusing only on the negative aspects.

There is research indicating the positive value of stress. Although high-level stress and tension are bad for emotional, physical, and mental health, an absence of tension and stress is equally unhealthy. Dr. Hans Selye developed a theory on eustress and distress.[18] According to Selye, eustress is a normal, constructive reaction to responsibilities and insecurities that we face daily. It has a necessary and positive value in our lives. Tensions keep us in touch with reality. Communities, like persons, need tensions if they are to grow.

Sometimes provincials and other major superiors have been told by members of their communities that they cannot change anything about their present life-styles because such change would subject the members to tension. These religious have concluded that all tension is harmful. But the person who experiences no tension is, figuratively, dead. Tensions are inevitable and a fact of everyday life. The challenge is to learn how to deal with them effectively, i.e., to learn to make tension work for us instead of against us.

When a group of disparate individuals are formed into community, tension is a natural consequence. Community tension provides the energy necessary to remain in the state of pilgrimage. Tension challenges the community members to change, to grow, and to reach beyond their present level in a continual response to the ever present call of the Lord. A true Christian can never remain static.

Tension may be coped with in either an adaptive or a maladaptive manner. Maladaptive behavior is present when religious act out their tension by means such as drinking or engaging in genital activity. More often religious engage in fight or flight responses. In some communities, all meetings are characterized by unresolved active or passive fighting. Members need to identify the source of the tension and determine whether fighting is their corporate way of dealing with it. In other communities the flight syndrome is more evident: people simply *don't* deal with one another. The communities in flight exist in a nonverbalized life-style of live and let live. Literally, community members withdraw from one another and engage in only the most superficial conversation. They avoid anything that might produce tension. Consequently, they avoid growth.

Familiar and adaptive responses to stress include concentrating on things such as prayer, our relationship with the Lord, friendships, support groups, enjoyment of esthetic values and activities, and sports.

9. *Members accept the group's norms.* George Bach's study of groups shows that when members participate in establishing the group norms there is not only a greater cohesiveness among the membership but also more likelihood that members will accept and feel a commitment to them.[19] Most congregations are already aware of this fact and are attempting to develop structures that allow members to be more involved in setting the direction of the community. Often this has been done with skill and foresight, resulting in a greater degree of potency and responsibility among the members. At times poor handling has produced great pain and stagnation. Unfortunately, involvement has become an end in itself rather than a means to reach the ultimate end of all communities, i.e., mission. The criterion for success must be the degree to which participation fosters and enables mission to happen.

Acceptance of group norms in the local community needs to be addressed on an annual basis. Frequently norms are established for one group with no recognition given to the fact that the group and circumstances change. Group members need to be involved in developing new norms or they will not feel a sense of ownership and commitment to them. Development of norms is related to the in-out stage of group development described in Chapter 2.

OTHER PHENOMENA THAT AFFECT THE GROWTH OF GROUPS

Size. A question frequently asked in the course of workshops is, "What is the ideal size for a community group?" Researchers have suggested the ideal size for therapy groups, but we know of no similar research that indicates the ideal size for a community group. There are a number of variables to be considered; primary among these is defining the purpose of the group. Once this has been clearly articulated, the size most effective for achieving that purpose must be determined. Usually this can be stated in extreme limits rather than as a definite number.

Some people function better in smaller groups and some in larger groups. We have seen people who experienced great trauma and stress living in small communities, but who became very effective when they were reassigned to larger communities. Conversely, we have seen people regress in larger communities and flower when assigned to a small community.

Some researchers have discovered that three persons is one of the most difficult sizes for a group because of the potential for triangulation. Two-against-one situations develop and are difficult to handle. However, a group of three cannot be ruled out; when members are aware of the potential conflict and discuss it in their community meetings, like many other problems, it can be anticipated and alleviated.

In his research on children in groups, Herbert Thelen offers some observations that may have relevance to us in community.
1. The smaller the group, the more time there is available for testing ideas directly through overt participation.
2. The smaller the group, the less clearly defined the problem has to be to be able to work on it.
3. The smaller the group, the greater pressure each individual feels to participate, and the more visible is nonparticipation.

4. The smaller the group, the easier it is to express intimate thoughts and feelings.
5. The smaller the group, the less are its potential resources but the greater is its motivation.
6. The smaller the group, the greater the influence of each individual, including the "blockers" and "wreckers."[20]

Composition. Perhaps more important than the size of the community is its composition. Again Thelen provides some insight: "In general, the simplest way to express what is required to organize subgroups for most achievement-related tasks is that the members be well enough aquainted that they can communicate fairly readily; that there be enough range of temperament that they challenge each other; that they have among them enough skills of group process (socialization skills) that they can work together; that they have enough resources and enthusiasm for the achievement problem that they keep going on; that they have a secure enough role in the total group that they do not waste much energy comparing themselves to or belittling the other subgroups."[21]

Much of what we might say about composition has already been covered in the section on the conditions contributing to the growth potential of the group. A few comments, however, are in order.

During the past few years, there has been a good deal of experimentation with community groupings. From our experience we have developed the following theory: The more homogeneous a group is, the faster it arrives at simple task solutions but the less likely it is to deal with more complex tasks. The more heterogeneous a group is, the longer it takes to be able to work together to solve even the simplest tasks, but the rewards are great. However, in the long run, the heterogeneous group is usually capable of achieving much more than the homogeneous group. Conflicts arise from the diversity, but they can provide the impetus for creative solutions.

As much diversity as possible should be encouraged, since diversity allows for the greatest good to be accomplished, provided that the group can work together. Diversity mixed with a basic respect for one another is probably the ideal composition. However, that diversity needs some limits.

Every group has the potential to absorb only a certain number of neurotic or underdeveloped people. There is no magic formula for determining this number, but observation of the group will usually reveal when the group is approaching its limit. When this limit is reached, the group usually becomes destructive to all of its members.

Another aspect to be considered under the heading of group composition is the group's sexual makeup. Does it make a difference that communities, generally speaking, are all one sex? Are there differences between all-male and all-female groups?

We have already stated that the dynamics that are at work in one group are present in all groups, regardless of the purpose or composition. Yet the responses or reactions to these dynamics are frequently influenced by the group's composition. Our observations on sex as a factor, though clearly generalizations, are offered so that others may compare them with their own experiences.

In men's communities there is often a great deal of resistance to entering into dialogue. Perhaps it conflicts with the macho image many male religious feel they need. Men tend to use humor more frequently in their meetings. At times this creates a comfortable and relaxed climate. At other times it is used to avoid dealing with difficult issues.

When conflict finally emerges in men's communities, it is approached more directly than in women's communities. And once it has been dealt with, men seem better able to leave the meeting without bringing the conflict into their daily living situation. In contrast, the conflict between two or more members in most women's communities seems to be remembered longer and more intensely and to interfere with the community growth.

Women appear to be much further ahead than men are in developing successful communities, if the abilities to share faith and to dialogue on a value level are used as criteria. Women seem to be comfortable with an affective relationship with God in a way that men frequently aren't. This is especially important when we consider that in the bishops' study of the American priest, one of the differences discovered between those who remained and those who left was that those who stayed reported a more affective religious experience.[22] Women also seem better able to share their dreams, hopes, and other nonthreatening areas

of their lives. Both men and women seem to have difficulty sharing their fears and failures.

Women seem to be more sensitive to the needs of others in the
community than men are, but they are also more easily hurt because of this sensitivity. Frequently women experience hurts and
rejections that were never intended.

As a general observation, women seem to be more indirect in
the way they deal with things, especially with potential conflicts.
This creates an ambiguity that increases the tension of the group.

Women tend to do more subgrouping than men do. This is
often seen when friends gather after a meeting to discuss what
happened. These subgroupings tend to reduce the level of trust
that the group needs for its growth.

We would also like to say a word about our observations of a
coed therapy group of religious in ministry. The men and women
in this group were able to talk with one another at a level they
were not able to achieve in their own communities. They raised
questions that helped to dispel myths they held about their own
or the other sex. Mistaken assumptions on which they based their
previous behaviors were corrected in dialogue.

On the basis of our experience, we have developed a bias. We
know that living together in coed communities is not a viable
option in the near future, but we feel more opportunities need to
be provided for men and women religious to meet and dialogue
in a limited, nonthreatening manner.

One other element recommended by Thelen is that members
of communities possess group process skills sufficient to carry
out their tasks. It has been our objective throughout this book to
insist that group skills are essential for growth as a community.
Skills cannot be learned just from reading a book or from attending a random workshop in communication. Communities need to
give serious consideration to providing group skills as part of
their initial or ongoing formation if they consider community
living to be one of their priorities.

BARBED WIRE DISEASE

In ending this chapter we would like to introduce a unique phenomenon, "barbed wire disease," first identified by A. L. Vischer

in prisoners of war in World War I. Vischer found that all the prisoners were motivated by the same basic need to preserve their identity. The symptoms common to the syndrome included the following: "Many of the prisoners combine fault-finding with a passion for declaring themselves superior to their neighbors; . . . [this] gives rise to extreme irritability so that they cannot stand the slightest opposition and readily fly into a passion. A mania for discussion develops, but sound judgment is entirely lacking in the argument."[23]

As we read this, we were struck with the way it paralleled many community meetings we have witnessed. The last sentence especially reads like a parody of the stereotyped community meeting, i.e., discussion abounds but sound judgment often seems to be lacking.

When a community tends toward a closed system, i.e., one in which members expect to have all their needs met by one group of persons with whom they live, we might expect to find this barbed wire disease. As was mentioned before, communities that function as closed systems are self-destructive.

Members should expect to have some of their needs met within the community. This is why they belong. They believe they can grow and be more effective in ministry because of the supports they receive from the community. If, however, they are trying to use only one group as their sole support system, like the prisoners just described, they will become preoccupied with the struggle to preserve their identity.

Communities must become open systems, in which some needs are met within the community and others are met outside. People have sometimes been made to feel disloyal if they sought some of their support from outside the community. Rather than weakness or disloyalty this is a sign of health. For the well-being and health of both the person and the community, open systems need to be encouraged.

When community meetings are characterized by a mania for discussion without apparent sound judgment, two questions need to be asked: Are people struggling to preserve their identity? Is the community becoming a closed system?

The prisoners of war developed barbed wire disease, but they were trapped. They had no options. This is not true of us in communities. If we are trapped, it is because we have chosen to be trapped. The option is always available to us to use resources outside the community. If we fail to do so, the blame lies with us.

CONCLUSION

Hopefully, the material in this chapter has provided an increased understanding of community. As you caught glimpses of your own community, it may have brought a grin or a frown to your face. If the effect was a grin, glory in the humor inherent in community life. If the effect was a frown, determine what you must do to assist your community to grow.

Everything that has been discussed in this chapter implies that good communication produces growth in communities. Poor communication, on the other hand, will increase the frustration and the pain. In the next two chapters we will focus on how to improve communication in community.

NOTES

1. Merle M. Ohlsen, *Group Counseling* (New York: Holt, Rinehart and Winston, 1970), p. 96.
2. Jerome D. Frank, *Persuasion and Healing* (Baltimore: Johns Hopkins University Press, 1961), pp. 262–289.
3. Rudolph Dreikurs, "Group Psychotherapy from the Point of View of Adlerian Psychology," *International Journal of Group Psychotherapy*, 1957, Vol. 7, pp. 363–375.
4. Ohlsen, *Group Counseling*, p. 91.
5. *Ibid*, p. 82.
6. Charles B. Truax and Robert R. Carkhuff, *Toward Effective Counseling and Psychotherapy: Training and Practice* (Chicago: Aldine, 1967), pp. 121–143.
7. John Powell, *Why Am I Afraid To Tell You Who I Am?* (Chicago: Argus, 1969), p. 113.
8. Marjorie Kellogg, *Tell Me That You Love Me Junie Moon* (New York: Farrar, Strauss, 1968), p. 176.
9. Irving Yalom, *The Theory and Practice of Group Psychotherapy* (New York: Basic Books, 1970), p. 38.

10. *Ibid,* p. 41.

11. W.J.H. Sprott, *Human Groups* (Baltimore: Penguin Books, 1970), p. 27.

12. Dorwin Cartwright, "The Nature of Group Cohesiveness," in D. Cartwright and A. Zanders, *Group Dynamics: Theory and Research* (New York: Harper & Row, 1968), pp. 91–109.

13. Dorothy F. Beck, "The Dynamics of Group Psychotherapy as Seen by a Sociologist: Part I. The Basic Process." *Sociometry,* 1958, Vol. 21, pp. 98–128.

14. Herbert Kelman, "The Role of the Group in the Induction of Therapeutic Change." *International Journal of Group Psychotherapy,* 1963, Vol. 13, pp. 399–432.

15. Yalom, *The Theory and Practice,* p. 40.

16. Kelman, "The Role of Group Psychotherapy," p. 410.

17. Erik Erikson, *Childhood and Society* (New York: Norton & Co., 1963), pp. 247–251.

18. Hans Selye, *Stress Without Distress* (New York: Signet, 1974).

19. George Bach, *Intensive Group Psychotherapy* (New York: Ronald Press, 1954), pp. 344–361.

20. Herbert A. Thelen, *Dynamics of Groups at Work* (Chicago: University of Chicago Press, 1963), p. 63.

21. *Ibid,* pp. 63–64.

22. National Opinion Research Center, *The Catholic Priest in the United States: Sociological Investigations* (Washington, D.C.: United States Catholic Conference, 1972), p. 314.

23. A.L. Vischer, *Barbed Wire Disease* (London: John Bale and Danielson, 1919).

IV

Communication in a Caring Community

In the preceding chapters we have looked at some of the dynamics that affect community living. In the next two chapters we will focus on the issue of communications.

Chapter 4 will present some general information on communication, and Chapter 5 will provide information on skills that can be used to improve communication among community members.

COMMUNICATION AND COMMUNION

Communication occurs whenever people are gathered together in a group. It consists of verbal and nonverbal networks, and it keeps members of the group in relationship. It is through this network that members exercise a positive or negative influence on one another. Communication in communities is never an end in itself. It is intended to foster communion among members through the sharing of feelings about common experiences and values. Communication and communion involve risk and trust.

When communication evolves to true communion, we are in the process of developing a caring community.

Each of us becomes a more complete person through loving and being loved, that is, through relationships. Religious community is nothing less than the network of relationships among persons who experience a mutual call to the service of the Lord. Communication is at the heart of this network and can therefore mean life or death to a community. No community can grow and accomplish its mission of witness unless its members are communicating and in communion with one another.

Sigmund Freud wrote, "No mortal can keep a secret. If his lips are silent, he chatters with his fingertips; betrayal oozes out of him at every pore."[1] Our silences are full of nonverbal behaviors: eye contact, hand gestures, facial expressions, physical appearance, and dress.

Communication may be intentional or unintentional. Intentional communication takes place on the conscious level; we have a goal to achieve, and so we wish to get our message across to the other person to accomplish the goal.

Unintentional communication operates at the unconscious level. Whether or not we know it and whether or not we like it, we are always giving messages to others. Just by our presence we project either a concern for others, which encourages them to live and grow, or we transmit our indifference, hostility, or aggression, which communicates our indifference. Unintentional communication is exemplified in the embarrassing slips of the tongue and uncomfortable forgetting of names at a crucial moment.

Each of us has only to look at our personal experiences of being misunderstood or misquoted to know that communication is difficult. As one person cleverly put it, "I know you believe that you understand what you think I said, but I am not sure you realize that what you heard is not what I meant."

Most messages involve both content and feeling. Children unconsciously pick up the feeling of the person speaking. Gradually, as children gain control over vocabulary and become more fluent, they tend to pay less attention to the feeling of the speaker and become more dependent on the verbal content of the message. Socialization enables persons to become adept with words to the point that they use them to cover up or deceive others. Such verbalizations can become so refined that they even fool the person employing them. But they don't fool the listeners or observers. Either the nonverbal behavior gives the speaker away, or at best their behavior is not congruent with their verbal messages. This leaves the listeners confused. Have you ever been at a meeting in which some people sit through the whole session and say nothing and later claim that they had no influence on the decisions made? And yet you remember them sitting with arms folded, eyes downcast, and unresponsive, while dominating the meeting through the discomfort and anxiety they created in other group members. Meanings are conveyed in many ways. Words may be symbols but their meaning is found in the person who speaks and the one who listens.

BLOCKS TO COMMUNICATION

Each of us, as we responded to God's call to community, packed our suitcases and landed on the community doorstep. We soon had our possessions unpacked and stowed away. The "invisible baggage" each of us brought, the acculturation from our childhood and adolescence, was less noticeable. No one helped us unpack the multitudinous patterns of behavior that we had acquired in coping with our physical, psychological, and spiritual needs. These patterns may have been appropriate and effective in getting our needs met, or they may have been inappropriate and ineffective, but they were the only patterns we had. We knew no other ways. We tended to judge others by the only standard we knew, our experiences. When others' patterns of behavior, expectations, role definitions, etc., coincided with ours, we felt secure. When patterns were unfamiliar we were uncomfortable. Inevitably, this affected our ability to communicate, especially when we found ourselves on completely different wavelengths from others.

Let us look at some of the "baggage" we brought from our past and how it influences our communication in community. We have classified it under five general headings: images and expectations, anxieties, defense mechanisms, language, and purpose.

Images and Expectations. The images and expectations we hold flow from our experiences and are therefore unique to each of us.

BLOCKS TO COMMUNICATION IN COMMUNITY

Images
expectations
anxieties
defense mechanisms
language
purpose

It is a common mistake to assume that others have the same images and assumptions we do. In working with communities of religious, we have found this accounts for much of the distrust. Persons live side by side in parallel monologues, missing each other completely. They pass judgments on one another without realizing that the other person's perception of a situation is quite different from their own. As an example, if one priest comes from a family background in which affection is expressed openly and frequently, he would probably respond warmly to those who greet him with an open display of affection. He would feel comfortable. In contrast, the priest coming from a family in which an overt display of affections was considered inappropriate would probably feel uncomfortable in the same situation. Perceptions and expectations have been learned. The person who expects to be hugged will feel puzzled and rejected when met with a stiff response or a hand formally extended in greeting. Each person makes a judgment on the other in terms of his own familiar background.

Families have unwritten rules related to their values. One of these pertains to illness. In one family a headache is cause for great concern and much tender loving care. In another family a headache is a sign of weakness and should be denied or ignored. Translated into community living, these differing values create problems. The person expecting attention and sympathy will be hurt and confused by the seeming indifference and rejection of companions who are embarrassed by what they see as the weakness of the sufferer.

Our families have taught us how to see ourselves. The person with great self-confidence and a sense of worth may find it difficult to be sympathetic when, or to understand why, another person feels worthless, dependent, and diffident. Families determine attitudes toward authority. How we feel about leisure time and its use also stems from family attitudes.

Our past sets up our expectations of the present. Self-fulfilling prophesies are often the consequence of our own expectations. If we expect people to like us, we will no doubt act in such a way that they will. If we expect people to be trustworthy, they will probably turn out to be so; if we expect people to take advantage of us, they probably will. We set up the conditions to bring about the behavior we expect. When we find ourselves distrusting another person for no apparent reason, we might dialogue with ourselves to find out why. If we can find no rational basis for our feelings, we may need to reflect on our family experiences to find some basis for our irrationality. Unconsciously, we have absorbed family patterns in acting and reacting to persons and situations. These patterns are carried over into community. Communication will suffer if we use these irrational bases for making judgments on others.

Anxieties. Anxiety is a subjective emotional response to any situation that is perceived by us as an unnamed threat to our well-being. It interferes with communication because it diminishes our ability to perceive the situation or person accurately. If our perception of the reality is inaccurate, the behavior that follows will probably be inappropriate and ineffective. A certain degree of anxiety is normal to growth and does not hinder a person from carrying out responsibilities. We may feel a mild tension before meeting some important person or undertaking some project. This is a normal reaction to something that appears to threaten our existence as self. Every person experiences normal anxiety on many occasions in the course of development and confrontation with the various crises of life. For example, the new candidate entering religious life will feel anxious about the host of unknowns he or she will encounter.

Neurotic anxiety is anxiety disproportionate to the real danger and arises from an unconscious conflict within the self. Most neurotic anxiety comes from unconscious psychological conflicts rooted in some earlier threatening situation that the individual did not feel strong enough to face. An example of this can be seen in the person who had dominating, possessive, or unloving parents but who repressed the problem. It returns later as an inner conflict producing neurotic anxiety (e.g., in a sister anxiously trying to win the approval of superiors when she is in fact trying to win the approval of her parents). Guilt is a frequent concomitant of anxiety, and so a vicious circle is set up in which anxiety leads to self-fulfilling prophecy of failure, which leads to hostility, which leads to guilt feelings, which lead to greater anxiety and tension. Threatened persons take refuge behind self-protective masks for fear of revealing themselves. Fear of reprisal keeps them from disagreeing. To be candid or to disagree might mean having to face anger and conflict, which they don't know how to handle. Distrust increases anxiety and anxiety increases the fear of losing identity. Those filled with anxiety cannot face the challenge to grow. All available psychic energy is needed to cope with known and even unknown threats to their being. The anxious person may resort to use of defenses such as denial, projection, and displacement, or the person may become a workaholic and put pressure on everyone else to do the same. Anxiety is a sign that an inner struggle is going on. It can be a healthy signal for us to uncover the causes of conflict and find an effective solution or way of coping. The aim is not to free ourselves entirely from anxiety but to use its energy in a positive direction, accepting what cannot be changed and changing what can and needs to be changed. In the words of Saint Theresa's Serenity Prayer as the criterion for action:

> God, grant me the serenity to accept the things I cannot change, the courage to change the things I can, and the wisdom to know the difference.

Defense Mechanisms. Defenses are tricks of the mind that keep us from seeing what we don't want to see. When we use defenses, we are kidding ourselves and escaping the truth. Defenses are unconscious, and all of us occasionally use them to screen out information we don't want to deal with. When defenses are used extensively among members of community, facts are distorted and communication is disrupted.

There are many kinds of defenses, but we generally use those we learned in our particular family patterns. As children, we developed unconscious processes to help us work out our problems and satisfy our needs. At times these processes were effective and at other times they may have kept us from realistic solutions.

Since defenses are a part of our daily lives together, we will select a few of the most common ones and describe how they operate and influence our communication and communion together.

Denial of reality. Denial of reality is the simplest form of defense. It is characterized by a person's refusal to face painful thoughts or feelings. It is distinguished from lying in that lying is a conscious process and denial is unconscious. In using this mechanism, the individual turns away from facing personal failures and faults. A sister who sees herself as always in control is very threatened by a sudden feeling of anger. The strong feeling challenges supposedly secure self-knowledge, and she feels something has to be done about it. Her first impulse is to deny the feeling because it is inconsistent with her way of thinking about herself. She responds, "No, I'm not angry," Of course, it is likely that this statement will be made in such a clearly defensive tone of voice that the anger is revealed to the listeners. The content or words say no, but the tone says yes. A double message is conveyed and the listener is confused as to which is real.

Other examples found in community life include the deaf person who refuses to admit a hearing loss or the religious who believes that a change in ministry would bring an end to all current difficulties. Denial consists of falsifying reality either by convincing ourselves that it does not exist or by perceiving it in a distorted way, both of which result in a more pleasant picture of the world. We can escape the need to face reality by procrastinating, by getting sick, or by keeping away from a situation in which we might fail or be criticized.

Rationalization. A commonly employed defense, rationalization is the justification of opinions or actions by fallacious reasoning. It means giving good or plausible reasons instead of the actual or real reasons. The good reasons excuse us from making an adjustment or accomplishing a task. Since it is self-deceiving, rationalization is potentially dangerous; it is used to disguise or hide unrecognized motives.

Blaming is another form of rationalization. The sister who says, "I can't get along with her and nobody else can either" is putting the blame on the other person without examining her own behavior. Her reasoning supports her own perceptions. If we find others to blame for our lack of success, we can simply proclaim our frustrations and avoid correcting our behavior. Rationalizers will always invent causes beyond their control. In this way they are safe.

The essence of the rationalization lies in finding self-satisfying reasons for what we do or say. The explanation protects us from the anxiety that would arise if we allowed ourselves to face the inconsistencies present in many of our actions. Rationalization fools only the rationalizer, and it is very difficult to deal with persons in religious life who have ready-made explanations for everything. Rationalizations cover up a lack of growth and keep us from truly coming to terms with our real personalities. They keep a community from open and honest dialogue since they cover up what's really going on inside us. When our defenses are up, we reject criticism and insist on our own explanatory tales. Rationalizations can be signs of serious trouble since they indicate an inability to face the truth. Neurotically defensive persons keep patching up the fabric of a self-created world. They're always the good guys, the misunderstood heroes, the saints, or the victims of everybody else in the community. In a religious community characterized by openness and trust, these people can be helped to face themselves by others who are gentle but refuse to accept the rationalization. Adequate self-knowledge with acceptance from others helps those who are happy to accept themselves the way they are. They are aware of their feelings and reasons for actions and don't distort them out of some neurotic need. They are able to assess their strengths and weaknesses, knowing what they can and can't do. They are able to set realistic goals for themselves, neither underestimating nor overestimating themselves in the face of life's tasks.

Personal, affectionate relationships with other people are the foundation of an accurate self-knowledge. There's no denying the benefit of friends who are truly interested in us and who love us enough to confront us with either our shortcomings or our unfulfilled possibilities. When we begin to hear what our feelings are telling us and are able to express these feelings, we begin to understand ourselves and life. To be able to face ourselves is to be able to make use of the real experience of our lives and to make these experiences readily available to others.

Arguing with people who rationalize only encourages defensive reactions, since it forces them to protect their position. The best way to help these people is to help them identify and associate with others who are able to face reality and who feel no need to justify their behavior by resorting to rationalization.

Regression. As a defense, regression involves a retreat to an age-inappropriate behavior to avoid responsibility or demands from others and to engage in self-indulgence. It is a childish response used when we are confronted by difficulties or problems that seem too big to be faced. Regression can be seen in persons indulging in temper tantrums or uncontrolled emotional expressions. Probably the most common form of regression is withdrawal. Withdrawal does not necessarily mean increasing physical distance. Sulking behavior is a form of withdrawal. Children learn that they can run away from an unpleasant situation by crying or looking very sad, while at the same time punishing the family. The parents' efforts—"Show me a smile" and "Now don't cry"—may sometimes be successful, but they result in reinforcing the withdrawal behavior and it becomes a relied-on tool. Children learn that adults are tuned into reading their moods and that the moods can be used to communicate to their parents. Children also learn that they can use moods without being held responsible for them. They come to believe that the mood is not under their control—that they are victims of their own moods. Sulking pays off. Children can withdraw and feel they have been victimized, even though they indulge in their tantrums quite willingly and enjoy the effect on those around them. They find pleasure in conveying the message of suffering. Covertly, children communicate to the adult that the adult has failed them. The child is not consciously aware of the covert aggression in the message but the parent hears it.

The unconscious use of moods to control others is very often a skill maintained throughout a lifetime. Hidden aggression through withdrawal expresses two needs: the need to punish and the fear of being punished. Withdrawal behavior can punish others without revealing the willful punisher. The suffering that the person endures is a small price to pay for the size of the punishment administered to others. Withdrawal behavior gives the message that the person no longer wants to accept responsibility or to cope with problems. The person refuses to participate, even when decisions are necessary. Responsibility is shifted to others, yet the withdrawn person gains the advantage of not being recognized as the aggressor. In religious life persons may withdraw by keeping busy or simply by being silent. The community does not recognize the mechanism for what it is.

Becoming fully Christian in community involves learning to respond in a positive way. There is a difference between withdrawal techniques, which are disintegrative, and the love of solitude, which is spiritually healthy. People who are absorbed by escape dynamism are sensitive, lonely, and self-centered, and there is little cooperation with others. Persistent and deep inferiority feelings seem to be present. These religious may be unobtrusive and seemingly submissive, and they may go unnoticed for a long time.

Behaviors used by religious to escape unpleasant realities are subtle. Problems may be explained away by blaming outside sources, depressions are blamed on circumstances. When in others' presence, these religious may withdraw into fantasies and imaginative play that make them oblivious to the chatter around them. When engaged in conversation, the withdrawn religious speak of the happiness or good times of the past, subtly expressing a wish to be children again.

Displacement and projection. These two defenses are closely related. Displacement occurs when we transfer feelings aroused by one person or object to another person or object not responsible for the original feeling. These pent-up feelings are discharged on objects less dangerous than those that originally aroused the emotions. Displacement usually involves hostility, but other emotions are present as well. Fears, for example, may be displaced from the actual source to related situations, as in the case of irrational fears called phobias. A brother who is afraid of failing in his new ministry may develop a fear of elevators or something else that makes it impossible for him to continue in that ministry. The phobia enables him to quit the new ministry without the self-devaluation he might experience if he were to fail.

In projection we unrealistically attribute an objectionable tendency of our own onto another person instead of recognizing it as part of ourselves. We falsely see in others the traits or motives that are really our own. The brother who likes to dominate every situation may accuse others of always trying to dominate. If he has acted dishonestly in the past, he may voice the opinion, "You can't trust anybody," as he interprets glances, words, and gestures as signs of threat or dishonesty. Projection enables people to live more comfortably with themselves by seeing unwanted traits only in others.

Fear fosters an exaggerated tendency to project suspicions onto others. It fosters gossiping, continual rudeness, and tattling. Persons who project give themselves away by offering the same diagnosis of others once too often. In religious life those who lash out at others take the heat off themselves but make life difficult for everyone else. When projection becomes a habit, it blocks the climate of trust needed for communication and communion. Persons who use projection need to be supported in areas in which they can begin to feel competent and successful. A sense of competence enables them to accept themselves and their own limitations.

Reaction-formation. A person prevents dangerous desires and feelings from being expressed by exhibiting attitudes and types of behavior that are the direct opposite of the original desire or feeling, such as by stating, "I'm so happy," when actually the person is very sad. Other examples are excessive politeness, courtesy, submissiveness, amiability, and concern, which disguise underlying hostility, aggression, or death wishes. These operate, as do other defense mechanisms, on the unconscious level.

Reaction-formation is one of our most effective ways of defending ourselves against what is going on internally. We disguise our true motives or desires, since they could cause us guilt or shame if we admitted them at a conscious level. The person in community who does not truly feel committed to living the vow of poverty may become overconcerned with how everyone else is living it. Often the zealous reformers in religious communities are those persons who are afraid their own feelings may drive them in the opposite direction. The reformers insist just a little too strongly and the contradictions become obvious to others, although the person remains unaware of the problem. The over-zealous reformers often end up by misdirecting the lives of other people, finding comfort in reassuring themselves that they are only trying to do the Lord's work.

Reaction-formation, like other defense mechanisms, helps us to maintain socially approved behavior and protects us from the stress of acknowledging that we have antisocial or unethical desires. But the self-deception involved is not conducive to a realistic and effective solution of our problems, and the harshness with which we treat others shows neither understanding nor fairness.

Perfectionism. The priest who is unconsciously uneasy about doing something, even when it is important to get it done, may invoke this mechanism of perfectionism. He may keep holding on to whatever it is he is supposed to do, telling himself and everyone else that he hasn't got it quite right, that it needs a few added touches, that the times aren't right, or that he needs more information. The priest is playing the perfectionism game and buying time to protect himself from the possibility of conflict or criticism. Those who get caught up in this never get anything finished, because they are never completely satisfied with the product. It is actually easier on their egos to postpone things than to take the risk of making a mistake or allowing the community to see that they are fallible. Playing the perfectionism game, they never have to take a chance. No one can criticize them because they claim not to have done the thing to their own satisfaction. Talent is wasted and community members become impatient with the person who places impossible demands on himself or herself.

In addition to the unconscious defense mechanisms, several other defensive mechanisms constitute obstacles to communication in a caring community. These operate at a subconscious level.

Passive aggression is the psychological mechanism through which we hurt other persons by not doing anything at all. It is an indirect but extremely effective form of aggression. In passive aggression a response is withheld. By not showing up for a meeting we promised to attend, we can do more damage than if we had tried to express our aggression in a more obvious manner. Not talking to someone can be a passive way of expressing aggression. Passive aggression is usually a pattern of reaction that comes from the needs of a certain kind of personality. It describes a style of relating to other persons. Although passive-aggressive persons are not fully aware of what they are doing, they manage to do it very well. They have mastered the moves of subtle aggression, knowing just the moment at which to withhold support, just when not to answer a letter, or just when to drop out of a group. With all innocence, the passive-aggressive person can say, "I didn't do anything." In reality a great deal of hostility has been released to poison other members of the group.

Passive-aggressive persons are extremely difficult to deal with because conflict never surfaces and they are unwilling to cooperate. They manage to maintain a rather serene picture of themselves as well-controlled, proper, nonviolent human beings. But they are not the peaceful or loving personalities they pretend to be. When they are confronted with the disruptive nature of their style, they do not easily give it up. Often they remain remote and inaccessible to healthy relationships. If any relationship begins to build, the passive-aggressive person quietly withdraws, leaving hurt behind. Unfortunately, this personality is common in religious communities.

The *putdown* has become a style of relating in American culture. Hidden under cleverness, putdowns are really defensive masks to disguise the person alienated by loneliness. The tactic is to assert superiority by putting the other person down. It's a dangerous game in which others are kept at a distance by using jest to hide hostility.

People using putdowns seem to have a sixth sense for discovering the most vulnerable areas of others; they wound other persons where it hurts most, leaving them no way to fight back. Persons who use this style of relating will say, "I didn't know you were so sensitive."

Putdowns are most effective and most harmful in close relationships such as families or religious communities. The persons who use them are hurting and have learned to keep others at a distance with their verbal weapons. They claim they didn't mean to hurt, that they were just kidding, but the person who has been shot down feels attacked, isolated, and powerless.

Do-gooders practice another style of blocking communication by solving your problems for you. These people live with fantasies of rescuing people, solving other persons' problems, and saving the world. The trouble is that they are there when *they* want to be, not necessarily at the time you need them. The do-gooder is not a good listener but rushes about spreading rescue nets under our lives and getting in the way of our learning to cope with our own problems and living. These persons fulfill their needs by manipulating the lives of others.

The *self-wipeout* is also prevalent in our society and particularly in our religious communities. These persons depersonalize an experience by placing blame on an inanimate object, that is, by avoiding the responsibility for their own feelings. For example, instead of saying, "I didn't like the play or movie," they say, "The movie was dumb." Other examples are "It dropped out of my hand," instead of "I dropped it," or "The bus went off without me," rather than "I missed the bus."

The problem with using defense mechanisms is that while they may keep other people out, they also hide gifts we have to give. It takes time, trust, respect, and faith in others to eliminate defenses. They cannot be dropped overnight, and they should not be torn away. If we abruptly expose other people's defenses before they are ready to face them, they may never mature. Only as we outgrow our need for defenses can the defenses be dropped.

All of us use defenses. They become unhealthy and neurotic only when they are the main way in which we relate to life. Growth and openness develop gradually. As we come to trust one another, we don't need to use defenses to protect ourselves from hurt. We can risk reaching out to other persons even when our trust may be misplaced; we are prepared for this to happen occasionally.

Language. So far we have been describing the baggage—images, anxieties, and defenses—we bring to communication. We will now look at another block to communication in our communities:

language. Language is effective only to the degree that it brings about a meeting of meaning between two or more persons. Language is based on a set of symbols (words) with assigned meanings. Since words are always subject to the distortions of our emotional associations, meaning depends not only on words but also on the feelings behind them. Meaning is found in people. The adequacy of language is a function of human experience. We hear words and interpret them against our background of experience. Since each of us has a different background, each will hear different things. One sister announces to the group that she intends to sleep late the next morning. She is very annoyed when someone starts the vacuum cleaner at 9 A.M. What does late mean to her? What does it mean to others?

Language also depends on inflection and tone of voice. Vocal emphasis can greatly change meaning. Depending on how a sentence is spoken, a different message is conveyed. If I say, "I did not say you left the dirty dishes in the sink," I can change the whole meaning by placing the emphasis on different words in the sentence. "*I* did not say . . ." might imply that while somebody else said it, I did not agree. Or, "I did not *say* you left the dirty dishes in the sink" could mean, "But we both know that you did." The listener may hear something that is nowhere near what the speaker had in mind. When communicating we must continually ask for clarification.

In our efforts to communicate, we may concentrate on saying the right words and yet fail to get our meaning across because of the strong nonverbal messages. When people feel threatened, they can communicate an emotional static that drowns out their message.

Our experience with communities has been that communication on an intellectual level predominates; the feelings behind the words are ignored and viewed as unimportant. So often we hear, "Why don't people get things straight?" Much misunderstanding occurs because it is assumed that if we say the right words, our messages are bound to be understood. Since meaning is shaped by experience, a completely identical interpretation of the message would depend on an identical history among the participants.

Silence is another aspect of language. Just as the rests in

music are as much a part of the music as the notes are, so silences are as much a part of our language as the words we speak. Ultimate intimacy is often shared silence. Silence can communicate awe or the need to reflect and internalize what has been communicated. We can remember standing in awe before Michelangelo's *David*, fully aware that no words could express the feelings we were experiencing at that moment. To try to translate those feelings into words would have seemed almost sacriligious.

Silence can be a two-edged sword. It can be used to create a distance between persons, to avoid difficult or potentially painful situations, or to express hostility. Silence then becomes a block to communication.

We can never be absolutely sure of the meaning of another's silence. We may feel overwhelmed by awe and interpret the silence in others to mean the same. In truth, the other persons may be bored and feel that there is nothing to say. Failure to verify our assumptions can contribute to blocked communication. Some people have absolutely no tolerance for silences. Their need to prevent them from happening in groups can block real, intense communication. These people never allow others to take the necessary time simply to digest and internalize what is being said. On one occasion in which we were supervising a group leader and listening to a tape of one of his sessions, we asked him why he had jumped in so quickly during a pause in conversation. He responded that he felt a need to break the long period of silence. Thanks to the miracle of instant replay we could run the tape and let him time the long three seconds of silence! At times, even a few seconds of silence can seem interminable, especially when we are feeling anxious or responsible for the group's conversation.

Language can be revealing or concealing. It reveals only if we desire communication and are willing to work hard to achieve it. In another section we will discuss at greater length the part that feelings play in communication.

Purpose. The fifth block to communication is the motivation or purpose of each communicator. When two or more persons enter into a conversation, there is an implicit assumption that each intends to listen to what the other is saying. We have only to look at our own experiences to realize that this assumption is ill-founded. How many times have we heard persons arguing angrily and vehemently and suddenly realized that there was no real point of disagreement? How many times have we found ourselves formulating a rebuttal when we have heard only the other person's opening statement? Some religious seem to need to contradict or disagree regardless of what is said.

Purpose is closely related to listening. If I enter the communication intent on hearing the what and why of the other persons, I will disengage myself from my immediate concerns and try to listen from their point of view. If I do not understand, I ask questions to clarify their position. Whether or not I agree, I want to understand what the other persons are saying and how it concerns them. When the sole purpose is to prove a point regardless of what is said by others, the situation becomes one of self-assertion. There is really no interaction, even though the persons are physically together. It is a conflict situation in which one person must win and one must lose. The intent is to make the others admit that we are right, which means that they are wrong.

The point of communication should be to share insights so that we can come closer to the truth. When fear of change makes us unwilling or unable to listen, then communication is blocked and truth cannot be found. The purpose of communication must be to gather information that will enable us to make responsible decisions based on facts rather than on emotions, and ultimately to bring one another into the presence of God's truth.

In summary, the ability to communicate can be blocked by the things that go on inside of us, i.e., the images and expectations we have and the anxieties and defense mechanisms we use, and by the blocks presented by language and purpose that exist between ourselves and those with whom we seek to dialogue. Being aware of these blocks and working to overcome them will facilitate the ability to interact through dialogue, a goal of the caring community.

DIALOGUE AS A MODEL FOR COMMUNICATION IN COMMUNITIES

Community is accomplished through dialogue. Communication becomes dialogue when we share ideas, make choices, give and receive knowledge or advice, or solve problems. Dialogue entails constant movement toward the mutual understanding of one another through the sharing of feelings, ideas, and beliefs. There is no need to justify these since in dialogue there is an acceptance of the integrity and worth of others. What really matters is our genuine acceptance of the uniqueness of other persons and our willingness to respond to that uniqueness. When our own message becomes the central focus without concern for the response or reaction of others, we are engaged in monologue.

Dialogue develops the ability and confidence we need to reach out to others in a loving relationship. It enables us to move out of our stagnant relationships and begin to know our own inner richness and the inner richness of those with whom we live. We begin to unfold as persons.

Paradoxically, while we yearn to experience dialogue, we are anxious and fearful of the intimacy that such dialogue brings. We build walls and hide behind them to protect ourselves from hurt and rejection. Religious may live together for years and not get beneath the superficial differences, idiosyncracies, and failings that keep them from communion.

Every person is called to enter into relationships with other persons. This is part of our humanity. Through our entrance into a particular community, we give others permission to know us, to influence us, and to challenge us. They cannot do this unless we present ourselves sincerely, say what we believe and feel, and remain open to the words of others. Dialogue is a combination of the processes of self-disclosure and feedback. Each will be discussed separately, but together they bring about self-knowledge.

Self-Disclosure. There are many things we can learn about others just by observing them closely. There is also a vast private world to which we have no access unless the other persons choose to reveal it to us. Self-disclosure is the process by which we freely share information about ourselves in a personal way. This information cannot be uncovered through any other source. It is our story told from "inside." It passes by all the factual descriptions and goes to the heart of the matter as we unfold our anxieties, aspirations, secret hopes, and broken dreams—the unique development of a personal past.

Self-disclosure is difficult, and we have many resistances to it. Telling it like it is may have been frowned on in our early lives. A display of emotions may have been punished as a lack of discipline. We may not have experienced any level of intimacy as children. In any of these circumstances we will have learned to keep our private worlds sacred from outsiders.

Sharing our inner lives can seem almost indecent to persons who have learned to hide behind masks or defenses. Self-disclosure can be an invitation to enter into an intimate relationship, and we may be afraid of the demands this intimacy places on us. To reveal ourselves leaves us vulnerable. It may result in a challenge to change and grow when we'd rather say, "You don't understand me," and retreat to an inner safety. To be rejected by someone to whom we have revealed ourselves is a much greater threat than being rejected by someone with whom we have created a distance.

Why take the risk? Because our individual call to community is a call to share with others, to take on mutual responsibility for one another's lives as we witness the presence of the Lord in the world today. We cannot do this if we live as strangers. We must support one another.

Self-disclosure is not an end in itself. It is directed toward building relationships that will provide the support we need to be more effective in using our gifts in ministry to further the Kingdom.

Self-disclosure does more than allow others to know us. It helps us to know ourselves. Carl Jung says that all human beings have a vast "undiscovered self" that they need to get in touch with.[2] To know ourselves not only takes courage but also requires the help of others. As we tell others of our secret past—our thoughts, feelings, needs, and vulnerabilities—they can give us feedback that helps us to be more objective. Our self-knowledge increases, and we can let go of our defenses. We do not have to hide from others. The energy used to maintain our defenses can now be invested in living.

How much we want or need to disclose about ourselves is an important question. How much to disclose depends to a great extent on the purpose of the group. A group of religious meeting to talk about the quality of their lives together would probably expect more self-disclosure from members than would a group of persons who did not live together. But living together between meetings may make self-disclosure a greater risk. Persons vary in their feelings about self-disclosure. There are overdisclosers and underdisclosers. If one person discloses too much too soon, the group may feel they are being imposed on and resent the demands they feel the disclosures make on them.

The underdisclosers tend to create distance in relationships. By revealing too little, they maintain strict control, managing to appear emotionally self-sufficient even when they are not. An important factor in any self-disclosure is whether or not it is appropriate to the situation and purpose of the group.

Appropriate self-disclosure is part of an ongoing relationship. It has nothing to do with the instant intimacy established between strangers meeting on a plane or in a bus terminal. While these strangers pour out their stories in great detail, there is no risk of or responsibility for one another. Generally, self-disclosure begets self-disclosure. Both parties recognize that they are involved in an ongoing relationship. Self-disclosure is appropriate when it takes into consideration the state of the listeners. What effect will the disclosure have on the receivers? What demands does it place on them? Can they handle the underlying demands at this time? The discloser must give thought to the amount of information to be revealed, the intimacy of the information, the amount of time available, and whether the psychological state of the listener can sustain it.

Ordinarily, self-disclosure is appropriate when it grows with the relationship. Over a period of time relationships deepen. Appropriate disclosure does not overburden the listeners with information beyond their tolerance level.

While relationships are built through self-disclosure, there are times when some people will want to hide their reactions to the present situation. This may be an exercise in prudence. Self-disclosure would be inappropriate if the listener is known to be untrustworthy. It would be foolish to self-disclose to a person who has in the past misinterpreted, misquoted, or overreacted to disclosures. Silence in such a situation seems more appropriate.

Appropriate self-disclosure is a social skill that many persons find difficult to learn. Our public self conceals from others the brokenness, loneliness, and fears that we may wish to share in the hope that others may minister to them and provide us the freedom to be ourselves. When we cannot reveal ourselves to others, we often engage in behavior that has the effect of a smoke screen placed between our real self and others. But this behavior arrests our personal growth, since the quality of life depends on the effectiveness of our interactions with others. If there is no one who understands and accepts us in our brokenness, we experience loneliness and isolation. When we are accepted, we become capable of dealing with our own reality.

Self-disclosure is nurtured in a climate in which we feel safe. While self-disclosure opens us to the healing touch of others, it may also leave us vulnerable to the arrows of anyone looking for our Achilles' heel. When persons have taken the risk of self-disclosure they need to be affirmed. Group members may not agree with what is said, but they need to make it clear that it is the idea and not the individual that is being rejected. Openness deserves openness if we are going to develop close relationships. The way the group responds to the discloser's risk taking will be important for building trust in the group.

While religious need to disclose themselves for their own good and for the growth of the community group, they have a right to the privacy they need if they are to maintain their psychological, physical, and spiritual well-being.

We have an obligation to respect the privacy of each member. This is often disregarded in communities. A "what's yours is mine" attitude or a lack of discretion in discussing absent members violates the personal space each of us needs. This becomes doubly important when members engage in self-disclosure. Many religious have been burned when they opened themselves and became vulnerable to those they live with. Communities will never be able to sustain the dialogue needed for communion without setting a high priority on respect for the privacy of each member. In fact, without privacy a community cannot survive.

Privacy is not necessarily tied to a physical location. It may be found in a group of individuals who share the same personal values and ideals and with whom we can be ourselves without fear of external sanctions or criticism. Usually this is a small, intimate, and self-chosen group.

Feedback. Feedback, the second requirement of dialogue, is a process by which persons give us their observations on, feelings about, and reactions to our behavior. The objective of feedback is to transmit reliable information to the receivers so that they will be able to change their behavior if they desire to do so.

Each of us needs to be able to give or to receive feedback from others. A first step to giving feedback is to be able to describe accurately for ourselves the behavior we observe. Most of us listen routinely and pay little attention to gathering careful, objective data. Secondly, we must work at perceiving the behavior without trying to interpret the motives behind it. Motives are private and can be known only if others choose to share them. The third step is to present our observations precisely and objectively so that the receivers may compare our perception of their behavior with their own perceptions.

The feedback must be given in such a way that it does not result in defensiveness; when it arouses defenses it becomes useless. The objective is to give feedback so that others can hear it, understand it, and use it.

There are several guidelines we can use to minimize others' defensiveness in receiving feedback and to maximize their potential to use it for personal growth. Feedback expressed in specific rather than in general terms is better understood. For example, the brother who is told he is a pushy person does not know exactly what behavior is being reacted to, so he cannot change it even if he desires to. When the feedback is specific, the receiver is left free to choose what to do with it. "You are late and I feel annoyed" is a message that can be understood. The receiver knows what has been done and how it has affected the other.

Effective feedback focuses on behavior that can be modified or changed. If the behavior cannot be changed, calling attention to it only leads to frustration for the receiver. Some behaviors are easy to change and others can be more difficult. How much success there will be depends on the strength of the person's desire to change. It may be useful to ask whether the receiver perceives the behavior as modifiable.

Feedback that is imposed will not have the same effect as feedback that is solicited. When a person asks for feedback, there is a greater willingness to hear it. If it is imposed, it may be the sender's need that is being met rather than the receiver's. Imposed feedback is more likely to arouse defensiveness, which defeats the purpose of the feedback. Feedback that is solicited is more likely to be received in trust and acted on.

Feedback must always be motivated by a concern to help others grow. It should take into account the readiness and willingness of the recipient. There is no place in genuine dialogue for feedback intended to hurt another person.

Feedback related to events in the past is less effective and less constructive than feedback related to immediate concerns. Feedback given in a group has the added benefit of being evaluated by more than one person. Some groups have regularly scheduled sessions for giving feedback. It would be helpful in this situation to review the guidelines for giving useful feedback.

Finally, effective feedback is non-evaluative. It is directed toward the behavior without any judgment of the person's worth. Someone acting in a boorish way is not necessarily a boor.

Sometimes when we give feedback we feel disappointed or angry when it is not put to use. No one can be forced to change, the motivation must be internal. It may be that the sender's feelings and expectations need to be looked at. Group members may continue to confront those who persist in behavior that is irritating to them. Those from whom change is requested must accept the consequences of their refusal. This may mean living with group disapproval, but the responsibility for change lies with the individual.

Feedback is a valuable part of communication because it helps us to know how we stand in the eyes of the community. All of us at times wonder how other people see us, whether we belong, etc. Through feedback we can learn how our behavior affects other community members. Do the members share our perceptions of the way things are? As we observe others and ourselves in the group, we can compare and contrast their reactions with our own. In doing this as a group, we come to establish norms and standards of objectivity.

Each community has goals to be met or achieved. When we look at our behavior as a group, we can get information about our performance and progress and check it against our desired goals.

This kind of feedback stimulates individual members and the group to new knowledge and behavior. On occasion, sharing feedback with each member of the community can stimulate changes in feelings and attitudes of the whole group.

The process of dialogue, giving and receiving feedback, is not easy. It presumes caring, trusting, acceptance, openness, and concern for others. However, being difficult is not the same as being impossible. Dialogue is a means of helping members of a group achieve their goals.

DEVELOPING AND MAINTAINING TRUST IN COMMUNITY

Trust is a basic ingredient of both personal and communal life. We can't grow unless we receive it, and we are not really mature unless we can give it to others. It is that extraordinary quality that enables us to make space in our lives for other people and to let them see what we are really like. At the same time trust allows us to see others as separate from ourselves and in need of freedom to be themselves.

The human heart searches for someone to trust. Trust is an easy thing to talk about but a hard thing to give. It is easier to protect the heart from hurt by not trusting.

The hallmark of Christian trust is the continued concern and support we offer to others even as we keep ourselves available and vulnerable to them. The crucial elements in this trust are openness and sharing on the one hand and acceptance, support, and cooperative intentions on the other.

Openness has to do with the ability to share information, ideas, thoughts, and feelings as well as reactions to issues that the group is pursuing. Openness can be helpful or harmful, effective or ineffective, and appropriate or inappropriate depending on the person's motives and ability to be sensitive to the effects of sharing on the recipient. It implies responsibility for the other person's ability to receive our confidences.

Sharing is the ability to offer our materials and resources to others to help them move the community group toward accomplishing its goal.

Acceptance is the communication of high regard for other

persons and their contribution to the work of the group, i.e., communicating to members an appreciation of who and what they are.

Support is focused on getting across to others your recognition of their strengths and your belief in their ability to manage well the situation challenging them.

Cooperative intentions indicate the expectation that we will behave in a cooperative manner with other group members to achieve the goals of the group.

All these elements may be present even while we express disagreement and opposing points of view. Trust is violated by those who are open without thought of their impact on others, e.g., pouring out feelings at inappropriate times or displaying insensitive "sensitivity." Trust is violated by persons who place inordinate value on telling it like it is without concern for the feelings of the recipients.

Early in the life of the community group, people tend to be closed and to program their communication carefully. They plan what they will say and control their communication through impersonal statements such as "People need people," instead of making more personal statements like "I need you."

Creating a climate of trust is the most important task of the new community group. Little can happen until the members learn to trust one another. Since all the members of a community have been drawn together by a common call, it seems that trust would be a natural consequence. This is not the case.

Creating a climate of trust entails members declaring themselves in the group, that is, declaring their honest feelings. Someone has to take the risk of initiating this. It takes an act of faith to get up the courage to entrust ourselves to others, since there is always the risk that they may not accept us. Paul tells us that this is the way of the Lord: "Men of Corinth, we have spoken to you frankly, opening our hearts wide to you. There is no lack of room for you in us; the narrowness is in you. In fair exchange, then (I speak as a father to his children), open wide your hearts." (II Cor. 6:11–13)

When the trust level in the group is low, the members' behavior becomes more impersonal, closed, determined by "should's," and more dependent. When the trust level is high, the behavior of the members is more personal, more open, more self-determining, and more interdependent.

Low trust level makes it difficult if not impossible for members of the community to deal with conflicts; they are reluctant to talk about conflict for fear of destroying the group. If there are signs of distrust, then this should be brought out into the open and confronted. Is there some specific behavior that is making trust more difficult?

One way to begin building trust is to take time to acknowledge aloud the good qualities of each member of the group and the constructive relationships they have with other community members. During a meeting, all the members should take turns speaking about the good personal qualities and strengths they have observed in others. Following each person's contribution other members of the group should add the strengths they have observed in the speaker. When all members have had a turn at this kind of affirmation, the group then focuses on the community as a whole. Members of the group brainstorm a list of good things that are happening in their local community. When they have identified and publicly affirmed one another's strengths and the strengths of the house as a whole, they may then begin to raise issues that need to be talked about to further personal and communal growth.

The process described above points up some components of building trust. As we assist other members of the community in recognizing their strengths and in receiving communal affirmation, a positive atmosphere is created and the level of safety in the group is raised. Second, through this exercise members are able to focus on the things they have in common. Third, the exercise encourages each person to share feelings and be heard on a nonthreatening level and to hear others in the same way.

Trust building begins when members feel good about themselves and can identify points they hold in common despite disagreements. Trust building occurs when people in a conflict can affirm their opponents and break down the stereotypes of the opposition. This affirmation is often followed by informal talking, which helps to reinforce trust. Sometimes when conflict cannot be resolved a third party must be brought in to initiate trust building in the group.

"To each person the manifestation of the Spirit is given for the common good." (I Cor. 12:7) Trust involves risking ourselves in all our weakness. Each of us alone is weak, but called together by the Lord we are strong. Cement, which holds houses together, is made of sand, lime, and water. Each of these elements alone can easily be blown away or lost, but put together they form a strong substance that can weld stones together against the forces of nature.

The catalyst for welding together the strengths of each community member is the development of skills of self-disclosure and feedback in an atmosphere of mutual trust and faith.

NOTES

1. Sigmund Freud, *Dora: An Analysis of a Case of Hysteria* (New York: Collier Books, 1905) p. 96.
2. H. A. Illing, "Jung on the Present Trends in Group Psychotherapy." *Human Relations*, 1957, Vol. 10, pp. 77–84.

V

Practical Aspects of Communication in Community

In Chapter 4 we discussed various dynamics of communication as they affect our community living. In this chapter we will look more closely at some practical aspects of dialogue and communication.

Dialogue may be defined as an exchange of ideas through open sharing, or the consideration of the pros and cons of an issue to discover the truth. We often assume that we are dialoguing, but dialogue is difficult and more rare than we think. Dialogue requires more than skill; it requires a mastery that comes only through patience, time, and a real desire to communicate. Learning the skills for dialogue is a first and necessary step, but a conviction of its need and value provides the motivation for the effort required to create a climate of dialogue.

We will look at the following six important elements related to dialogue and discuss how each influences our life in community: feelings and emotions in general, anger as a special emotion to be dealt with, listening ability, confrontation, management of conflict in community, and some ground rules for communication in a caring community.

FEELINGS AND EMOTIONS IN GENERAL

Feelings are an ever present part of our lives. They give flavor to our relationships. Trouble comes not because we have emotions but because we try to pretend that they don't exist. When we ignore feelings, we lose contact with them and therefore lose control over them. No matter how much we distort, repress, ignore, or disguise feelings, they still exist.

Feelings tell us what we like and dislike, what we need, and when to back off and look at what is happening to us. Brother P has been feeling tired and depressed. He can ignore his feelings and become methodical about his ministry. He may repress his feelings and become insensitive to those of others in the community. He may lash out at another brother as if he were the cause of his depression. Or he may try to get in touch with what is going on inside himself, the feelings that he doesn't like in himself and cannot accept, e.g., anger. Until he can recognize his own feelings, he cannot deal with the depression he is experiencing.

Sister J prides herself on being as rational and self-controlled as a calculating machine, moved only by ideas. Unconsciously, she sets herself up for trouble. Though she is unaware of her feelings, her emotions go on stimulating and twisting her insides. She is a victim of her unacknowledged emotions. The intense headaches she experiences before every board meeting are ascribed to all sorts of reasons and handled by taking aspirin. She cannot admit to the "weakness" of anxiety, anger, or fear.

A community meets to accomplish important agenda. The group works hard but can't seem to get the task done. Ideas brought up seem to bounce around the room and get lost. Members are becoming frustrated and angry. One person suggests that the group stop and look at what is happening, but another member says, "We can't waste time talking about how people feel. We have work to do." Persons or groups may tell themselves that feelings have no place in their work, but the work continues to be stalemated. Words flow articulately and profusely, but little communication takes place. On observing such a community group, we might imagine that while dignified, mature conversation seems to be in progress across the table top, great bowling balls roll beneath. Fixed smiles and polite words deny and ignore the pain being inflicted on unseen ankles and shins under the table. Nothing much can happen in the group until the members deal with the war under the table. The unacknowledged pain robs the members of the energy needed to get the task completed.

Much time spent in community meetings is wasted when emotions are not recognized and allowed to surface. If decisions are reached, they are often implemented only half-heartedly, if at all. A general rule for meetings is to stick to the designated task until the feelings get in the way, then deal directly with the feelings until people are free to reinvest their energies in the topic at hand.

Coping with emotions and feelings involves several steps:

1. Allow ourselves to be aware of what we are feeling. If we have ignored our feelings over a long period of time, we may experience difficulty in identifying them. If we can substitute the word think for the word feel, we are not talking about feelings. We should observe our interactions with others. Feelings of low intensity are more difficult to identify, but they are present. Sometimes another member of the community or a friend can help us identify our feelings. If we ask them for feedback, we have to be willing to accept it, reflect on it, and perhaps later ask for clarification of their observations. Others are often able to tell us what we don't know about ourselves.

2. Admit our emotions or feelings. We must learn to identify our emotions or feelings by name. If we are feeling affection for someone, we should admit it. Often it can be very affirming if we tell the other person. We should talk about the meaning of our feelings for both of us. When we are feeling anger, we must honestly identify it and not use some term that seems more acceptable, e.g., annoyance. Some emotions such as jealousy, anger, and guilt are difficult to accept in ourselves. We should reflect on the feelings and become realistic about having them before we dialogue about them.

3. Explore our emotions. We should try to trace where the feeling is coming from and how it developed. Emotions are auto-

matic reactions to stimuli and are closely related to our value systems. Investigating the source of the feeling and relating it to our personal beliefs can lessen its intensity. Sister M realizes she is furious with the retreat director but doesn't know why. She begins to piece together the puzzle and discovers that in the last conference the director challenged a private belief she has retained from a childish spirituality. She feels terribly threatened, anxious, and insecure. Her way of dealing with her feelings is to become furious with the person who is challenging her belief system and therefore threatening her security. When she investigates her feelings and traces them back to their source, she is able to understand her emotion.

4. Tell someone about our emotions. Without blaming anyone, we should report the facts. Feelings come from within, so no one can make us feel anything. Our reactions are our own. All of us like to find a convenient scapegoat to blame for feelings that we don't want to accept in ourselves.

Father G celebrates the liturgy and Father R becomes upset because he feels the liturgical celebration is too legalistic, a perception based on his own expectations and feelings. Father G cannot be blamed for Father R's feelings, since other persons are finding the same liturgy as satisfying as any they have ever attended. The feelings are in the person and not in the situation.

5. Integrate our emotions. The final stage in the process of coping is to determine how we wish to express our emotion. We are in control; therefore, our actions can be chosen to suit our own image of ourselves. Those people who have integrated their emotions with their intellect are not blown about by feelings. The mature person has self-possession and acts rather than reacts.

If we follow this process of observing, identifying, and investigating nonjudgmentally before we act, we will find that we have greater control over the expression of our emotions. The process may seem drawn out, but if it is used when emotions are intense, it gradually becomes a habit of mind that governs the way feelings are dealt with. As with all growth, it is a long-term project.

ANGER AS A SPECIAL EMOTION TO BE DEALT WITH

While all emotions need to be expressed in such a way that the person reconciles feelings with intellect, anger seems to be a special problem for religious. Sister S says, "It's not nice [i.e., Christian, mature] to get angry with another person. We must love everyone." Father T says, "If I expressed the anger I feel, it would wipe out our relationship." Or Brother J puts it this way: "It wouldn't do any good anyhow. It won't change anything." Each of these individuals is using rationalization to avoid dealing with anger.

The target of our anger is usually someone or something we care about, including ourselves. When we fear that our anger is irrational and destructive, we may try to conceal it, but this doesn't take the anger away. Anger can be redirected but never instantaneously eliminated. When it is not expressed, it becomes dammed up and can be disguised in a number of ways, including anxiety attacks, depression, lingering guilt, extremes in eating, escape through sleep, or inability to sleep. Dammed-up anger finds expression in physical illnesses such as ulcers, high blood pressure, consistent stiff neck, or sore muscles. It turns into self-sabotage when the person becomes accident prone, drug addicted, or self-derogatory. In other words, anger not dealt with constructively becomes destructive and manifests itself in ways that are ineffective, inappropriate, and psychologically and physically unhealthy.

Anger is a basic human emotion experienced by all people. It arises in response to a real or imagined threat to ourselves and when we experience frustration of unmet needs or expectations. How we handle anger differs according to our personalities. Some persons explode, others simmer, and others kick themselves. Our culture does not encourage the expression of anger in natural and creative ways. Self-control is often thought to be equivalent to self-paralysis, or to the ability to pretend we have no feelings. The constructive expression of anger is actually an art.

The anger cycle has a definite pattern. First, we perceive a threat to our well-being. Second, we automatically make assumptions internally about the degree of danger that the threat poses. Third, we measure these assumptions against the power we feel we have to deal with the threat. If we conclude that we can handle the threat, the cycle ends there. If we decide that we are powerless to deal with it, the cycle continues and we strike out in anger to destroy or reduce the personal threat and to protect ourselves.

As with other emotions, dealing with anger requires that we

stop, look, and listen to ourselves and the way we are reacting. It is important that we claim anger as our own without projecting it onto someone else. Owning the anger increases self-awareness and prevents useless scapegoating. Turning statements of blame into "I" statements locates the anger inside ourselves. For example, instead of saying, "You infuriated me by serving dinner so late," one can say, "I am angry that dinner is late and I will be late for my group meeting tonight."

Frequently the immediate object of our anger is not the actual source. We may be displacing our anger from a more threatening source onto a less threatening source or victim. For example, we may project anger onto the cook for being late with dinner instead of recognizing that the real source of anger is the pastor who assigned us to run a group at 7:30 in the evening.

Anger ranges from relatively mild reactions such as "I disagree" to intense reactions such as "I'd like to kill you." It is never an all or nothing experience. When we evaluate the level of our anger and assess it accurately, we increase our capacity to deal with it. "I am angry enough to quit my job when the pastor assigns me to something he doesn't want to do."

Anger happens when we assume that the situation is dangerous to us. Usually it happens so fast that we don't know why the situation is frightening. When we evaluate it, we may find that the threat is really only a minor difference of opinion or a relatively mild threat to our own bloated sense of self-importance. We must ask ourselves what we stand to lose. For example, "I realize that if I refuse to take this evening group I may lose my job. This job is important to me because I care about the people I serve and to lose this job would mean that I could not serve this particular group of persons."

Talking our anger over with a trusted friend is helpful. When the threat is shared, the internal anger cycle becomes an external, interpersonal situation. Shared anger diffuses the intensity of the feelings and clarifies our perceptions. It is helpful to have others we trust give feedback about our feelings.

Since anger is a reaction to a threat, we need to defend ourselves and still get our needs met without lowering the self-esteem of the other person or damaging the relationship. The constructive expression of anger follows the same rules as for other emotions. Expression must be an appropriate and accurate disclosure of our feelings about the other's behavior. It must be a concrete, specific, nonevaluative description of the behavior as we see it. The negative effects of the other's behavior on us must be described concretely. In the case of anger over the pastor's giving us the 7:30 P.M. group meeting, we might express it as "I feel angry and nonvalued when you give me assignments you don't want yourself, because I think you really don't care about me." This is constructive expression of anger because it gives the other person the opportunity to change behavior without losing face or becoming defensive.

Specifically related to the emotion of anger is the ability to forgive. To let go of the anger and cancel charges against the other person wipes the slate clean and frees us to begin new transactions. It is a magnanimous gesture and increases our personal power.

Dealing with anger can be discomforting, but when it is creative and appropriate, it leads to personal growth and improved interpersonal functioning. The anger cycle is complete when we can let go of our anger without a sense of losing face or self-esteem.

Anger in community life has two sides. To deal with our own anger is one skill, but to deal with anger in others is another. We may be taken by surprise when another person attacks us without any apparent reason. Our initial, spontaneous response is to prepare for fighting or fleeing, just as we would if we were physically attacked. When a person attacks us verbally, there is little value in trying to rebut. Whatever we say will probably be misconstrued because anger distorts perceptions. Thus, if someone is angry with us, it is particularly important that our own communication be especially precise and accurate.

In most cases the precipitating incident is not the original source of the anger. The sister who launches an attack has probably been long involved in conditions that provoked it. She may be experiencing frustration or a sense of worthlessness and failure. She directs her anger toward us because we are safer targets.

Father G attacks Sister T for reasons she can't identify. A closer look reveals Father G's reaction as a displacement of his anger provoked by a group he feels has rejected him. If we understand some of the reasons for the inappropriate anger, we can respond more to Father G than to his inappropriate anger.

The more in touch we are with our own anger, the more likely we are to be able to deal with it in others. The following observations should be considered when handling others' anger.

• Being in touch with your own responses enables you to anticipate the ineffective response you might be inclined to give and thus forestall it.

• When others attack, the anger may be unrelated to the present situation. Remembering this helps you listen patiently and lets others know that you are trying to understand their needs. Their anger will become diffused as they express it and feel that they are being heard.

• Angry feelings need to spill out. As they flow freely, the anger begins to dissipate. Just talking is cathartic. To interrupt only rekindles the anger.

• Accept the right of others to be angry, whether you agree or disagree with the reason. Feelings are real, and as long as they are being expressed there is a certain integrity. Identity and personal worth cannot be tied up with your agreement or disagreement, they are separate from the anger expressed.

• Listen carefully to the anger and show by your attitude that you respect and affirm those expressing it. Through your nonverbal behavior, let them know you are listening and trying to understand. Nod affirmatively. Don't crowd or move in any way that might indicate anger on your part.

• Keep cool. Express your acceptance of the angry feelings; an angry outburst indicates that the issue must be important. Through your attitude, allow others to know that you appreciate the importance of their feelings.

• Keep the pain of the other in mind. Since anger is usually a reaction to hurt, either real or imagined, it is more beneficial to deal with the cause of the hurt than with the anger itself. If you can focus on the other's hurt, your own anger and anxiety will be diffused.

• Above all, remain silent until the angry person is ready to hear you. Silence when you are being attacked can be difficult but very rewarding. Respond only to the feelings that you have heard expressed. Do not try to justify yourself. Through your verbal and nonverbal behavior, let the person know that you recognize the importance of the situation and are sympathetic. This caring and concern can be communicated even when you don't completely understand the person's attitude.

• After listening, if you have been part of the problem, admit it fully and willingly. No reconciliation can take place if you cannot acknowledge your own responsibility. When action is needed, it is better to act than to sit around listening and sympathizing.

• Restore closeness with the angry person. This can be done by noting some positive element in your relationship on which you both can agree. This step is not just a technique. It is a way of restoring areas of common interest to be pursued.

• Communicate positively in setting up expectations that others can handle. Don't challenge them to the point that they feel frustrated and powerless.

• Anger must be dealt with. If we expend all our energy repressing anger, we will have little left to invest in love. We cannot be stifling feelings of anger and at the same time hope to be experiencing love. Anger and love do not operate in separate compartments.

When we can begin to deal with our own anger and to accept anger in others, as a community we are on our way to healing. Refusing to admit to difficulties may anesthetize the situation, but it will not resolve it. Anger will not be fixed by saying prayers and waiting for it to go away. Honest expression clears the air and brings problems out into the open so that the community can handle them.

LISTENING ABILITY

Listening is a process that brings us to the point of knowing what is going on in other persons' lives at a particular moment. It is more than a physical hearing of verbal messages. When a message is distorted, most of us tend to blame the speaker. We overlook the fact that communication depends as much on the receiver as it does on the speaker. Without a tuned-in listener, a message falls apart. Listening is not a passive act; it is an act of positive focusing of attention on the message being offered.

Listening requires attention, reception, and perception. At-

QUESTIONS TO EVALUATE YOUR LISTENING ABILITIES.

Do you put what you are doing out of sight and out of mind while you are listening?

Do you think about what is being said and try to understand what it means?

Do you try to understand the ''whys'' behind what is being said?

Do you listen regardless of the person's manner of speaking or choice of words?

Do you let others finish what they are trying to say, and if they hesitate, do you encourage them to go on?

Do you sometimes restate what was said and ask if you have interpreted it correctly?

Do you withhold judgment until the person has finished?

Do you really want to hear what others are saying, or is there something going on within you that prevents you from hearing?

tention is the process of selectively choosing from the environment the stimuli we will attend to. At the same time, we block out or ignore stimuli deemed not relevant. Some stimuli are given full attention while others receive partial attention. Attention is usually given to what will satisfy our needs. The relationship between the speaker and the listener will also condition the selection of stimuli and the amount of attention given.

Reception is usually a physical function. If the listener's hearing is limited by a physical impairment, the quality of the listening will be affected. However, reception is also influenced by the degree of attention that the listener chooses to give to the stimuli.

Perception is essential to listening. No matter how carefully the speakers choose their words, the listener gives meaning to what is heard. The listener tries to understand what the speakers are saying and why they are saying it. The good listener does everything possible to make sure the ideas are understood as the speaker intends them to be. This means trying to see things through the eyes of the speaker, keeping in mind that another's reality *is* what that person perceives it to be.

We have truly listened to another when we can answer the question, "What is going on right now in this person?"

Our listening abilities can be improved, but improvement depends on practice as well as on knowledge. We offer the following practical suggestions for improving listening skills.

Improving listening ability requires effort. To be effective listeners, we must evaluate how much our listening behavior is influenced by our ability to be selective in what we choose to attend to, our physical limitations, and how aware we are of the influence of our own experiences on what we hear others saying. Can we adjust our frame of reference to that of the speaker?

Listening ability is improved when there is a definite purpose for listening. Motivation will be colored by respect that we have for the person. The effective listener is convinced that the speaker has something of value that he or she wishes to convey. With this point of view the listener tries to hear the speaker's important message. If we believe we can learn something from this person, we ask questions: "What can this person tell me that I need to know? What worthwhile ideas are offered? How can I grow through what is being said?"

The effective listener waits to hear the full message before making a judgment on either content or purpose. But concentration is a difficult skill and a basic problem in listening. Our verbal output is about 125 words per minute, while our brain can deal with about 400 words per minute. Unless we have developed the skill of concentration, we will find ourselves taking side trips unrelated to the message at hand. We can fill in the gap between the verbal and mental rates by reviewing previous points, trying to identify the theme in a succinct phrase, etc. We may also engage in noting nonverbal cues, e.g., the speaker's facial expressions, the gestures, and the tone of voice. Effective listeners use the time to try to put themselves into the speaker's frame of reference. Attention to nonverbal cues gives us some information, but these cues must be confirmed through dialogue or subsequent information. Effective listeners try to draw as much information as possible from observation and from listening but do not try to interpret it.

Part of the ability to concentrate is not to remember every word said but to catch the main idea and the feeling that accompanies it. The listener who tries to remember every word can repeat it verbatim and yet miss the message.

Another difficulty in communicating is the difference between what words mean to the speakers and what they mean to the listeners. When the speakers and the listeners have had common experiences, communication is less difficult. Empathy is the attempt on the part of the listeners to put themselves into the speakers' frame of reference. This entails allowing their minds to become quiet—assuming nothing, drawing no conclusions, simply waiting to see where the speaker will lead. This disengagement might be likened to the way children listen to the present moment, while waiting for the story to unfold.

Attentiveness and empathy are creative abilities. They bestow power and are the key to rapport, understanding, and mutual love and trust.

Being quiet does not mean being completely silent. Good listeners will ask about things that they do not understand, but they will not suggest their own answers. They will point out discrepancies and may interrupt a compulsive talker. Rather than being an insult, this interruption shows that they are really listening and care about what is bothering the speaker. Compulsive talkers go on incessantly about trivia becuse they are afraid of talking about their real concerns. Their jabbering is just as distracting to themselves as it is to the listener. Questions directed toward clarification and better understanding can encourage the speakers and help them to make their points clearer. Listeners have the responsibility to ask for clarification when they are uncertain.

In any message there may be words that wave a red flag and elicit emotional reactions. These words lessen the objectivity of the message. The listener is likely to be caught up in feelings that throw a smoke screen over the message.

Learning to hear correctly is one of the most difficult things about listening. When Sister A criticizes us, do we hear it as an attack and start to fight back with angry words, or do we try to accept the criticism as well intended?

Another cause of distortion is the way that the message is delivered. It is possible to have an excellent message that can't be heard because of distracting mannerisms, flawed delivery, or unpleasant voice quality. The listener must be able to separate the content from the delivery.

Distortion is also common when the listener interrupts before the speaker has come to the end. The listener, reacting defensively, does not permit the speaker to make all the points or to give all the information.

Good listeners are few. Most of us try to be effective listeners, but our efforts are often counterproductive. We have been taught so much more about speaking than about listening. Listening to other people's problems or showing interest in what they are doing is perhaps the greatest area to practice charity in our communities and in the world today.

Listening has a strange and magnetic force. When people listen to us, we want to move toward them and to be with them. We unfold, expand, and come to life. To listen is to begin the healing process that we all need. Listening intently is an intimate act.

When we listen to another person, we satisfy some of our basic psychological and spiritual needs, such as acceptance, affection, and recognition. Being listened to by members of the community affords emotional support that we need to realize our self-worth. When others listen to us we feel valued and important.

By listening to members of the community express criticism, we permit them to release tension. By providing them with an outlet, we help them to move toward more positive attitudes and maturity. If we do not listen, their criticisms fester into discontent and can be detrimental to ministry as well as to the quality of community life. If we listen to other members of the community and try to understand their perceptions, we can help them to change. They can reveal all kinds of things about themselves when the listener avoids scolding, looking shocked, or preaching. As they begin to feel accepted and understood, they can stop being defensive and can risk change. When someone else accepts them, they can accept themselves, a prerequisite for change.

By listening we can decrease or prevent emotional illness. People in distress can often cope with their problem if someone will listen and let them share it. Listening is a better way to prevent emotional illness than using tranquilizers. Listening is the very essence of psychotherapy.

When we allow others to share their joys and sorrows, we alleviate their loneliness. We share with all humankind a universal loneliness, which is in reality a loneliness for God. "Thou hast made us for Thyself, O God, and our hearts are restless till they rest in Thee" (St. Augustine). However, we can do much for one another through sharing feelings of loneliness. When we listen we offer a precious and most valuable gift, a sharing of ourselves with another, a relationship of intimacy of sacramental value.

To listen to another person provides a means of growth both for the other person and for ourselves. Listening helps us to know ourselves. The person who listens enters into a relationship, a mark of maturity. Through relationships, we become involved in the world of another and get in touch with our own individual experiences, our sense of who and what we are, and our feelings about ourselves. Listening develops a sense of respect for others as well as a healthy respect for ourselves.

Listening helps us to understand others. As we learn to see things through the eyes of other persons, we begin to understand them as they understand themselves. In giving them the fullness of our attention, we let go of our own positions and put ourselves at risk of being changed. We may disagree with others, but when we listen we are walking in their moccasins and entering their world.

Listening helps us to pray and to grow spiritually. When we have learned to be open to other people, we carry this attitude into prayer. We are more ready to hear God speaking and to risk getting involved with others and their lives when we have left our self-centered world.

Listening is not easy. It requires mental and physical energy. It cannot be commanded. We don't listen because we are told to. It is not instinctive. Listening must be taught, learned, and practiced if we are to develop skill at it. The listener must want to understand what the speaker means.

Perhaps a true story will best illustrate the power of listening. A psychiatrist in a Veterans Administration hospital was assigned a Korean woman as a patient. He did not speak a word of Korean and she in turn only understood a minimum of English. The hospital did not have any therapists available who spoke Korean. The psychiatrist's only option was to meet a number of times a week with the woman and simply try to convey through his presence that he was trying to understand what she was saying. He was trying to listen and really hear her, in spite of the language difficulty. After a couple of months the patient's husband came to the psychiatrist to thank him for the growth he saw in his wife. In many ways this story epitomizes what listening is all about, and how freeing and therapeutic it is when someone else truly cares and attempts to listen.

CONFRONTATION

Ask any community what immediate image they conjure up when the word confrontation is mentioned and the reply will likely be "a bloody battle." Confrontation is often associated with people being out of control and brutally hurting one another.

Confrontation, as we conceive it, is nothing like this. If you break the word down, confrontation simply means to put in front. It is a method of placing the facts as we perceive them before others. Confrontation has often been an explosive thing in community because of the way it has been handled. We would like to suggest a method of confrontation that can lead to better resolutions.

The most important aspect of confrontation is the attitude and purpose of the confronter. What are we trying to achieve through it? Have we already made up our minds so that it merely presents our side of the story with no room for other points of view? When it is effective, confrontation must be perceived by others as a presentation of our perception of their behavior. We must show that we care about those we confront and are concerned about their welfare. The important attitude is one of caring. If the only message that comes through is "you had better change, or else," we guarantee it will be ineffective.

Who does the confronting is the second most important element. In the past, those in authority were expected to take on this responsibility. However, we have gradually realized that the most appropriate person is the one who has the best possibility of being accepted. Communities determine who will be most acceptable and effective.

The person chosen must be careful to present the facts as he or she sees them. Nothing is more frustrating than being confronted with secondhand information. If a person is confronted with "somebody said . . . ," the confrontation will be responded to defensively.

Advance preparation should include determining how best to convey the message that concern is the motivation behind the confrontation. Present the facts as clearly, honestly, and accurately as possible. It is important to clarify that it is the behavior that is seen as destructive and not the person. This approach combines directness with gentleness.

When the facts have been presented, it is necessary to solicit the other person's reactions. However, since the other person may initially respond defensively, time to reflect on what has been said should be provided.

One final point regarding confrontation. While probably no time is a good time for it, some times are better than others. Confrontation tends to be more explosive when either party is extremely tired.

The goal of confrontation is not to change others but to give them information that will help them change themselves. As we said earlier, growth results only when we choose to change ourselves.

MANAGEMENT OF CONFLICT IN COMMUNITY

The ability to deal with conflict and to use it for the constructive growth of the community becomes the dividing line between succesful and unsuccessful communities. In Chapter 2 we identified conflict as a stage in group development. Here we will discuss the nature of conflict, conflict strategies, and skills for resolution of conflict.

Conflict management involves diagnosing the nature of the conflict and using cooperative methods to move into the problem-solving stage.

Most conflicts can be considered as either conflicts of needs or conflicts of values. There is a conflict of needs when two brothers want to use the house car at the same hour to go to two different places. This type of conflict can often be resolved by emphasizing cooperation or joint use rather than competition. The brothers may bargain, negotiate, compromise, and come to a solution that allows both of them to achieve their purpose and to feel comfortable in doing so. Negotiation can be effectively initiated when Brother J states; "I have a problem. If you take the house car to go to your group this evening, I won't be able to keep my appointment at the provincial house, which doesn't have any bus line near it." This is more effective than saying, "You are a very inconsiderate, selfish person. You're thinking only of yourself and your own convenience." In moving to problem solving, it is necessary to recognize that there are other options.

Conflict of values is rooted in our systems of beliefs. Often what looks like a conflict of values is really a conflict of expression of values. Two priests may value religious life but disagree on how it should be lived. As one priest defends his form of expression, it may appear that he is attacking the value system of the other priest. In value conflicts the persons must go beyond their differences to find a goal that is acceptable to everyone concerned.

Conflict may be managed in several ways, including through majority vote or through railroading, in which one or more members force their will on the group. Both these approaches result

OUTLINE OF CONFLICT RESOLUTIONS

DEFINE THE PROBLEM: Think of a conflict you are having with another person. If possible, ask the other person to help you answer the following questions. If the other person participates, any answer *must be agreed upon by the two of you.* If the other person cannot or will not participate, answer the questions to the best of your ability.

- **How do you define the problem between yourself and the other person?**
- **How does the other person define the problem?**
- **What behavior of yours contributes to or represents the problem?**
- **What behavior of the other person contributes to or represents the problem?**
- **What is the situation in which the above behaviors occur?**
- **What is the *smallest* possible way to define the problem?**
- **What are the areas of difference or disagreement between the two of you?**
- **What are the areas of commonality or agreement between the two of you?**

DIAGNOSING CAUSES: This is necessary for both parties to understand what behavior is acceptable and unacceptable to each other so conflict can be avoided in the future.

- **As explicitly as possible, state the other person's behaviors that you find unacceptable in the conflict situation.**
- **As explicitly as possible, state your own behaviors that the other person finds unacceptable in the conflict situation.**
- **What events triggered the conflict?**

GENERATE POSSIBLE SOLUTIONS:

- **What do you need to do to resolve the conflict?**
- **What must the other person do to resolve the conflict?**
- **What are possible mutually desired goals for the resolution of the conflict?**

DECIDE ON A MUTUALLY ACCEPTABLE SOLUTION: This decision should include an evaluation of the effects of implementing each possible solution and an understanding of the need for cooperative interaction to take place as a result of the solution being implemented.

- **What is the outcome of implementing each possible solution?**
- **What cooperative interaction will take place as a result of each solution being implemented?**
- **What solution do the two of you feel will be most constructive?**
- **What are the strengths you can use to resolve the conflict?**
- **What are the strengths the other person can use to resolve the conflict?**
- **What are the criteria you will use to know whether the conflict has been resolved or not?**

IMPLEMENT THE SOLUTION
EVALUATE WHETHER THE SOLUTION SOLVED THE PROBLEM. IF IT DID NOT, REPEAT ALL OF THE ABOVE STEPS.
Is communication open, has trust developed, do participants feel friendly, is there any resentment toward the other person?

in complete victory for one side, which inevitably leads to resentment and more conflict. Another option is compromise. By teaming up, various members of the minority in the group form a coalition to help one another achieve mutually advantageous goals. In the United States Congress this is known as a trade-off. The trade-off usually has a short-lived success and results in more conflict once the scheme is discovered.

The best way of resolving conflict in group decisions is through the strategy of problem solving, in which consensus decision making leads to a final solution that is acceptable to all.

If the problem-solving strategy is to be used in conflicts of needs or values, the parties involved must trust one another and work to locate the source of conflict. The use of the combined energies of all the parties increases the likelihood of resolving the conflict. This strategy makes the best use of the talents and potentials of the participants for reaching a solution to which both parties can be committed. Constructive conflict results in increased commitment to a relationship, greater efficiency in ministry, increased self-esteem for members of the group, and satisfaction with the resolution of the conflict.

Skills for managing conflict can be learned. One of the first skills needed is the ability to recognize a potential conflict situation. Some conflicts among religious have existed for so long that they are no longer noticed. However, the feelings generated contaminate the climate of the community group. In many cases the situation could be corrected if it were recognized and forced into the open. Some examples of potential conflict include different expectations regarding the amount of time that members should spend with the community, the need for quiet times in the house, and the confidentiality that should exist regarding house matters.

Practical exercises for airing conflicts in community can be used to keep conflict from building up. At the beginning of a community meeting, five minutes (or more depending on the size of the group) can be set aside for members to engage in uninterrupted griping about things that are not going well in the house. This can include discussion of frustrations and minor conflicts. The gripes are stated without rebuttal, to be discussed at a later time. This airing prevents small conflicts from festering and be-

GUIDELINES FOR MANAGEMENT OF CONFLICT

Set a *specific time* and date.

Set a *time limit* on the conversation so that people or groups involved are not worn down by the length of the discussions.

Set a time when *participants are not tired*. Late at night is generally not the best time to begin conflict resolution.

Set *times for future meetings* to discuss the problems or evaluate decisions.

Define a process or the steps that need to be taken in order to resolve the conflict—Who talks first? For how long? Rules about interruption, sarcasm, gunnysacking, etc.

Decide about a neutral third party. Is one needed? Who would we like? Does he or she have the skill we need?

Plan to meet in a place that is safe and neutral for all persons involved.

Establish a limit to discussion so that the problem does not dominate all the other aspects of the people's lives.

SOME ASSUMPTIONS ABOUT CONFLICT

People's attitudes toward conflict affect how they act and behave in a conflict situation, how they handle their feelings, the process they set up to resolve conflicts, and ultimately the solutions that they select. *The following assumptions can greatly facilitate handling of conflict:*

☐ *Conflict is a natural occurrence.* It will always be with us. Our task is to learn to respond to conflicts in the most creative ways possible.

☐ *Conflict is one way that individuals and communities grow.* It is a process in which different viewpoints or actions struggle with each other, merge, and form new modes of human behavior. Conflict is an integral part of the change and growth process.

☐ *Conflicts arise because people believe they have incompatible goals.* Conflicting goals may demand either changed behavior or changed values.

☐ *Social structure frequently causes conflict.* This is due to the ways that relationships in a community are put together (or not put together).

☐ *Conflicts should be worked on as they arise.* The goal of conflict resolution is for the individuals involved to move toward a relationship in which they can develop their greatest potential.

☐ *Conflicts have predictable dynamics and cycles.* They can be regulated to minimize damage to individuals and groups and to maximize growth and benefits for all concerned.

☐ *Feelings are integral components of conflicts.* Feelings and rational thinking are not the same. *Feelings cannot be solved; issues and behavior problems can be.* We should not act on feelings without considering where the feelings come from and whether they coincide with our plan of action.

coming problems later. This practice is related to the first skill of conflict management—recognizing sources of impending conflict. After the five minutes the group may clear the air by switching to things that are going well in the house.

The second skill in the management of conflict is knowing how to avoid unnecessary and destructive conflict. It is important to distinguish between conflicts over needs and conflicts over values; the first are far simpler to deal with. In community life collisions of egos and perceptual distortions are inevitable. These involve feelings rather than issues. Defensive reactions used to cope with feelings of anxiety, hostility, and aggression can deflect the conflict to the wrong issue. A group decides to perform a communal act to express their identification with the poor. They end in conflict over the choice of the act and lose sight of the important value on which they agree, identification with the poor.

A practical exercise intended to uncover hidden needs and expectations can be helpful. This is best done at the beginning of the community life together. One at a time, members express their expectations of the group, their needs from the group, their strengths, and the tensions they feel with other group members. These feelings may be recorded in writing or shared verbally. After this has been done, the conflicts can be identified and a time for resolving them can be arranged.

Dealing with conflict at this early stage forestalls the misperceptions, hostilities, and polarizations that drain off the psychic energy of individuals as well as of communities. Briefly put, this skill might be phrased: don't allow a mole hill to become a mountain.

A third skill in managing conflict is related to timing. Tensions usually build up over a period of time and through a series of events. As feelings escalate, real issues become lost in the emotional vortex. At this point it is useless to focus on issues since persons experiencing intense feelings cannot be objective. They need to vent their feelings. Sometimes this can be accomplished by encouraging them to release their tension in a safe and separate place, alone or with a friend. The presence of a facilitator to help members recognize and express their feelings can bring a group to the point at which real issues can be faced.

Timing means getting persons to the stage where, having dealt with feelings, they can proceed to work on a solution that meets the needs of all concerned.

The fourth skill is the ability to use conflict in such a way that it results in optimal positive outcomes for all concerned. This requires understanding the options that exist for handling conflict situations and for working to move a group into the problem-solving strategy. The group defines the problem in terms of its needs and discusses all possible solutions. These are considered and evaluated until a mutually acceptable solution is reached. When this cooperative problem solving results in restoring peaceful relationships with increased commitment, the conflict has been used constructively.

The fifth skill in conflict management is the ability to move through the stages of problem solving by using effective communication techniques and evaluation processes. Conflict involves interpersonal relationships and requires interpersonal skills to bring about a resolution. These skills have already been discussed in Chapter 4 and earlier in this chapter.

SOME GROUND RULES FOR COMMUNICATION IN A CARING COMMUNITY

Commitment to attendance. There will always be emergencies or occasions when persons have to go out of town, but unless members of the community make a commitment to be present for scheduled meetings, it will be difficult to make progress toward dialogue among the group members. It takes time and presence to build community.

Confidentiality. Whatever happens in the group remains in the group. This is absolutely essential if trust is to develop. Persons will be reluctant to share at any depth if they feel that what is said will be reported from the housetops. To speak freely and honestly is always a risk. But the risk is minimized if there are assurances that what is said will be held in strict confidence. If there is reason to believe that this trust has been broken, the matter should be confronted.

At the start of the group, members should agree on what they expect of one another relative to the boundaries or limits of confidentiality.

Participation. Because each person in the group has insights and gifts that the group needs if it is to be effective, members have a responsibility to participate in group meetings. Once reluctant members have had the experience of successful participation, they will be more active in the group. If some members refuse to participate, the group may have to confront them on their responsibility.

Active Listening. Listening needs to be practiced. Eye contact with the person who is speaking or with the audience makes conversation more forceful. Paraphrasing what the speaker is saying and identifying the theme help the listener as well as the speaker. Paraphrasing need not always be verbalized, but it is helpful when there is any doubt that you have completely understood the speaker.

Appropriate Self-Disclosure and Feedback. As the group develops, members commit themselves to being open. It takes time to peel off the layers, but gradually members reveal their honest feelings about what is happening in the group and what it means to them. Members must also commit themselves to giving appropriate feedback when it is needed or sought. Through self-disclosure and feedback, members gently but firmly help one another to get in touch with themselves and to grow. This is not an encouragement for sensitivity or encounter groups. We are referring here to growth groups.

Members Speak for Themselves. In speaking, each member uses the personal pronoun *I* to describe feelings and experiences. This is more risky than making general statements such as "we all feel" or "you make me feel." Use of first-person pronoun puts responsibility on the speaker.

Speaking in the Here and Now. Since the group is a group only when members are actually together, the principal focus should be on the present, even though the event being discussed may have taken place in the past. The event is past, but the feelings are present as they are recounted.

Reporting Feelings. While members should speak for themselves, they should never assume that they know how other persons feel unless they ask them.

Responsibility for the Group. Each member of the group is responsible for what happens in the group. Nothing happens that the group does not allow. If one or two members act as if others do not exist, all members have the responsibility to intervene. If some persons do not know what is happening in the group, they have the responsibility to stop the group and find out; we can't participate if we don't understand. If at any time members feel that ground rules are not being observed, the group must be confronted and invited to look at their behavior and how it violates the group agreements. Observations of group or member behavior offered as direct, simple statements of fact provide a challenge to change in the direction of the rules agreed upon by the group.

Processing the Group. Periodically, group members should stop and ask themselves how their work together is progressing. This can be done at the end of a session together or when someone feels that the group doesn't seem to be getting anywhere. Members should make individual statements regarding their own observations and feelings about what is happening in the group. There are no rebuttals and all members of the group must participate.

SUMMARY

We have presented information about stages, dynamics, and communication. In the next chapter we offer suggestions for facilitators working with communities and for communities anticipating using facilitators.

VI

Working with Community Groups

This chapter is based on our experience of working as facilitators with a variety of community groups, male and female, young and old, active and contemplative, and all shadings between. We have two goals. The first, our primary goal, is to share our experience with others who find themselves in the role of facilitating community groups. By sharing some of our experiences, we hope to stimulate others to share their experiences and knowledge.

The second goal is based on our belief that if communities are to select and use outside facilitators, they must be educated in knowing what to expect. Facilitation of community groups is a relatively new discipline. In the sixties, a number of poorly trained individuals inflicted themselves on communities desiring to build better interpersonal relationships among the members.

How you read this chapter will depend on your objective. If, on the one hand, you are working with communities as a facilitator, we ask that you look critically at the report of our experiences and at our recommendations. If, on the other hand, you are a member of a community that is using or is contemplating using a facilitator, we suggest that you read with the discriminating eye of an informed consumer. Begin to develop for yourself some criteria for choosing a facilitator or for evaluating the person you are already using.

THE USE OF OUTSIDE FACILITATORS

When the suggestion to use facilitators is made to a community by one of its members or by someone in authority in the congregation, it is often interpreted as a criticism or an indication that there is something terribly wrong. The truth of the matter is that all communities could benefit from the use of outside facilitators. Being less than perfect, all communities have areas in which they need to grow. Our experience has been that the healthier communities are the ones that seem more willing to bring in facilitators. They realize that they are making progress in their development toward becoming better faith communities but at the same time are painfully aware that there are areas in which they have reached an impasse. They have struggled unsuccessfully while trying to move beyond the point at which they find themselves. Their own internal resources seem inadequate and they make a decision to bring in outside resources—a person or persons who can be objective and who possess the skills to help them take the next step in their growth as faith communities. This decision is often reached with difficulty. It requires a willingness to allow outsiders to see the group at their worst and to share their conflicts, their neediness, and their imperfections. It means asking others to minister to them in the same way they minister to others. In general, we are more comfortable in the roles of givers and ministers than in receiving others' ministrations.

In some cases the decision to bring in facilitators is not left to the group but has been made by someone outside the local community, such as the provincial. We have been invited to work with communities because those in general administration have encouraged, suggested, or demanded that they engage the resources of facilitators. In other cases, provincial or general chapters have decreed that each house in the congregation use facilitators to assist it in moving through a process in which the whole congregation is engaged, a process designed to bring about corporate growth throughout the congregation. While we have found it easier to work with groups that have decided on their own to bring in facilitators, with few exceptions we have also found success in those communities in which the decision came from outside. Often this means dealing with longer periods of resistance. However, since the drive to experience a sense of belonging and a supportive community is strong, the resistances are gradually dropped. Members desire improvement in the quality of their lives and thus, even while they resist, they are hopeful that something good will result. Living in a community fraught with tension and feelings of alienation, loneliness, and worthlessness is painful and results in an ambivalence about change. Members feel anxious about investing themselves, even though they desire a climate that will provide a richer and more satisfying experience.

Once the decision to engage facilitators has been reached, we recommend the following: The members come together to discuss bringing in the facilitators. If none of the group has had experience with or knowledge of facilitators, the Vicar for Religious, the staff from the area diocesan consultation center, or members from the area's religious or sisters' council might be asked to recommend a facilitator. If a high degree of conflict and of personality difference is already present in the community, this last option might be the best way to proceed. Conflict already existing can be a block to deciding on facilitators and, in fact, can be used as a reason against working with them.

Groups can go on interminably deciding whom to invite. This is an escape mechanism. A time for beginning with the facilitators should be determined and that deadline adhered to strictly.

When some consensus has been reached on the choice of facilitators, they should be contacted and invited to come to a community meeting for an educational session. This allows the community an opportunity to see the potential facilitators and to hear the philosophy underlying their method of facilitating. It provides a period of dialogue and exchange that can be valuable in assisting the facilitators and the community to decide on a contract of mutual agreement. It permits the more fearful members of the community to raise their questions and deal with their anxieties. The actual decision to proceed is better left until after

CHOOSING FACILITATORS
Are their attitudes toward community compatible with those of the members?
What is their training?
Do they receive supervision or consultation?
Do they favor interaction or a leader-centered approach?
Are they individual or group oriented?
Does their approach create an atmosphere conducive to free and honest discussion?

the facilitators have gone. The community then meets for the final decision.

During this initial session with the potential facilitators, the members of the community should be observing a number of things. Do these persons have an understanding of community that is compatible with the attitudes held by the members? If not, are the values of the members and the potential facilitators so much in conflict that there is no chance of working together in a mutual endeavor? What sort of training do these people have in working with groups, especially with community groups? Many fine mental health professionals are outstanding in their work on a one-to-one basis but have no training or expertise in working with groups. Some communities have brought in such persons with disappointing results. The skills and knowledge needed for working with groups differ from those for working with individuals. Do the facilitators get supervision or consultation? Working with community groups is difficult and complex and can raise unresolved, unconscious conflicts in the facilitators' own minds.

This is less likely to become a problem if the facilitators are receiving supervision or consultation.

Another point to be looked at in the initial encounter is the manner and style of the facilitators. Is the approach and methodology used by them going to create an atmosphere in which people feel free to talk, or will it inhibit people and raise the fears and tensions within the group? Perhaps the most important task of any leader is to help create a climate of free, honest discussion. Without this, the entire process is wasted.

Do the facilitators encourage interaction or do they encourage a leader-centered group? The style will probably reflect the basic belief of the leaders. Since the group must go on operating long after the facilitators have left, we believe that an interactive group is more productive and growth producing in the long run.

Are the facilitators individual or group oriented? We have a bias based on our experience in conducting many community groups and on our supervision of others engaged in facilitating community groups. Leaders who tend to focus on individual behavior rather than on the group process seem to lose sight of important dynamics operating within the community—dynamics that must be brought to community awareness if the group is to move beyond them. An individual-centered group approach seems to allow a greater amount of scapegoating, which is always destructive, not only to the person who is being scapegoated but to the group as well.

The leaders need to maintain an awareness of the group process, what is happening to each individual, and how the individual and group interact. For instance, the leaders might notice that the treasurer of the house becomes belligerent every time the discussion focuses on issues of money. They are also aware that the others react to the belligerency by withdrawing. Any intervention should focus on both reactions, what is happening with the individuals and what is happening with the group.

Once the community has met and spoken with the prospective facilitators, the question always arises about what to do if one or more community members refuse to attend the meetings. Our advice is always the same: If the majority of the group feels that these meetings are important for their personal and communal growth, they need to proceed with them. To do otherwise is to give one person or a small group of persons the power to deny the community members what they need to continue their growth as persons and religious. Ultimately, we stand alone before our God, accountable for ourselves. We cannot allow the fear or resistance of another to prevent us from obtaining what we require to grow into the productive persons the Lord is calling us to be. We strongly recommend that persons refusing to join the meetings be encouraged to attend the first educational session. In this way they will know that they are not being excluded but will also realize the inevitable alienation they will feel as the community grows together. These people should be free to make their own decisions; they can be encouraged to change their minds and be included at a later date.

In the dozens of community groups we have worked with, there has been only one instance in which a person chose not to attend the community meetings. The group was extremely creative in discovering a way to incorporate him, and ultimately he joined the group.

Past Experiences with Facilitators. Many religious have been reluctant to invite facilitators. Some of the reasons for this are rooted in irrational fears; however, in some cases real events have contributed to this attitude. Many facilitators working with communities, especially in the early 1960s, were sensitivity "experts." A psychiatrist who had to deal with the casualties of that period described these experts as members of the "make one, give one, teach one" school. Individuals with little or no training would attend a sensitivity weekend and then feel they were qualified not only to be the leaders of other groups but to teach others who wished to conduct sessions. These individuals left people with an extremely negative view of facilitators. Even more tragically, the work of these individuals left a string of casualties, people psychologically hurt by the experiences. As facilitators in communities we have heard horrendous stories about the effect of these experiences on communities and individuals. We believe that sensitivity sessions have some value for some people in controlled circumstances, but these are the exceptions. In general, sensitivity sessions were helpful to some and destructive to others. Scapegoating was rampant, and in some cases the victims have never been fully healed. We question the value of such an approach in a community in which people have a group history and will be living together in the future.

As we mentioned, some facilitators were well-meaning, individual-oriented professionals, but they were either ill-trained in conducting groups or utterly lacking in understanding of the human dynamics of community life. Methods that would be appropriate in other situations were not only inappropriate but often ineffective and destructive when used with communities. Issues and emotions were stirred up but often not resolved. Facilitators used to working with groups of strangers did not understand the necessity of working through and bringing closure to the issues and emotions raised. In many cases the group was in a far worse state at the end of the experience than at the beginning.

For all these reasons and probably more, many communities and individuals are highly skeptical and even fearful of inviting facilitators. We hope in the next section to present material that will change that perception and assist communities to see the great advantages in using the skills of facilitators.

SUGGESTIONS FOR FACILITATORS

As we stated in the beginning of this chapter, this section is intended to provide advice to facilitators as well as to make all community members better-educated consumers.

Some Basic Beliefs. Working with community groups is a necessary, satisfying, and difficult endeavor. It is necessary because most community groups need help to grow to their full potential. Only a community in the process of growing can truly bear witness to the values members share and hope to impart to others, a witness that tells the world that a group of people can live and grow together and be rooted in their faith in the living God.

Working with community groups is a satisfying task because the group leader is helping to develop authentic communities by creating a climate in which growth and healing can take place. Vatican II has emphasized the role of community in the life and growth of each Christian. Our experience has been that all other issues, such as authority and problems of sexuality, recede into the background when a strong sense of community is developed. When people experience life with a group that communicates care and concern, they no longer need to search for people, such as authority figures, to blame. This also frees them to discuss their struggles in developing as human, sexual beings. Once these personal issues are discussed, they become less of a problem.

Facilitators who have helped a community grow have in doing so touched the lives of leaders in the Christian community who will in turn touch the lives of the multitudes to whom they minister. Facilitating community groups is, then, an experience of freeing people to grow to their full potential in religious life and to minister to those who are in a position to influence the larger church.

Community groups are perhaps the most difficult type to conduct, since they are a hybrid of many types of groups. A community is not a family, not a group of people coming together simply to accomplish a task or to focus on a particular problem, not a group of strangers, as you find in therapy groups. In developing an approach for working with communities, elements from each of these different types of groups must be included. Since no research has been done on facilitating community groups and little has been written on this topic, the leader has a minimum of information from which to proceed.

Contracts. First meetings are critical. Much of the future success depends on the first sessions. The primary task of the first meeting is for the facilitators and the community to discuss expectations and negotiate a working agreement, or what we will call a contract. This contract reflects corporate agreement on these expectations. Leaders must be clear on the expectations of the community and must challenge members to verbalize their unspoken hopes for these meetings.

The following are essential elements in the negotiated contract: purpose, task, duration, frequency, confidentiality, and the role of facilitator and members. They are discussed in more detail below.

Purpose. Most groups never reach their goal because their purpose is not properly defined from the outset. If the purpose is not clear, the group simply rambles on; no one is sure about what has to be accomplished. Therefore, every group should have a clear, realistic, and shared purpose. It should be articulated in a simple and succinct way, avoiding the use of trendy phraseology, which means nothing to some people and has a variety of interpretations for others. Too often when we have asked communities what their purpose in meeting is, they have produced two single-spaced typewritten pages containing all the latest religious jargon.

The purpose must be realistic or the group will inevitably become frustrated. Often members express this frustration by the fight or flight pattern, in which they either withdraw from the group or become hostile. It is important to consider a purpose that the group can realistically achieve within the time and conditions allowed.

Everyone must agree on the purpose. When each one has a different idea of what the group is trying to achieve, much time is wasted in fulfilling the unexpressed and even unconscious agendas. Purpose, then, needs to be tested against the above criteria. At the start of the group, members should answer the following questions: Is the purpose clear? Can the group realistically accomplish this purpose in a specified time frame? Do we all agree on the purpose? Most groups choose a purpose that has something to do with improving the quality of their lives together.

Task. By task we mean what the group will do to accomplish its purpose. What task is chosen as a point of departure does not seem to make a great deal of difference, as long as people talk about what is happening in their attempts at living community.

A task frequently chosen is to discuss those experiences that facilitate or hinder the quality of members' lives together. When a community is dealing with a specific issue, the task may be more specific and directed. For example, when one or more new members are added, the group may need to set an explicit task, to discuss how effective they are in including new members.

We generally do not suggest assigning a topic or task for each meeting but rather recommend letting the community dictate the topic according to what is happening at that time. We are inclined to make two exceptions to this rule when the community needs a great deal of structure and when a clear, pressing issue needs to be resolved.

Duration and frequency. From the outset, the group should agree on how many times it will meet, how often, and for how long. This raises the commitment level of each group member. We will discuss this issue further in dealing with resistances.

We have found that a meeting longer than 1½ hours seems to be counterproductive, especially if it is held in the evening after a long, demanding, frustrating day in the apostolate. One exception exists when a community chooses to spend an entire day or weekend working together. When this approach is taken, it is best to hold the sessions in a milieu separate from the residence or ministry site. This eliminates the problem of interruptions, such as phone calls and doorbells, distracting members and making the process more difficult.

Confidentiality. If the matter of confidentiality is discussed at the outset, group members will interact more freely. The leaders should assure the group that they will not discuss what is happening outside the group except to discuss the process together to facilitate the group more effectively. Similarly, group members should agree on how much they will share among themselves between sessions.

Confidentiality in community groups is often more complex that it is in other groups. People are living together and it would be absurd not to expect outside discussion of intragroup experiences. An agreed upon level of confidentiality must be sought that assures that no one will be hurt by being quoted to people who are not members of the group and who don't fully appreciate the context of any segment of the dialogue. Assurances are needed that cliques will not form outside the group and reinterpret the meeting in a way that forces one or more members to feel alienated or scapegoated and that a climate in which all members know that what they say will not be used against them outside the group. Groups can never be successful unless each member has this sense of safety.

Role of Facilitator and Members. The facilitators must clearly communicate what they will and will not do. Being a facilitator is different from being a teacher. Facilitators must clearly define their roles as persons employing their skills to assist group members to better use their own resources to achieve the agreed upon purpose. In turn, the members are expected to be honest and open in discussion and to assume the responsibility for accomplishing the purpose. It is their group and their goal.

Use of Cofacilitators. We believe community groups are more effective if two leaders work together. Co-leadership provides two different perspectives of the same event. It also prevents the group from being caught in the unfinished business of a single leader.

Ideally, one of the leaders should be a religious and one a layperson; one should be a man and the other a woman. And they should work well together. The most important criterion is that the co-leaders be well trained in group leadership and in understanding community dynamics.

Resistance. Within any group a dynamic that is always operative is drive-defense. Earlier in this chapter we discussed the ambivalence of the members. Drive-defense is another way of describing this. The group members truly hope for a better quality of community life, but they fear that to achieve this they may have to give up some things that have value to them. Therefore, they resist moving toward the stated purpose. This fear will be different for each person, and the facilitators must help the group to confront it. Often the fears are more illusory than real. However, if they are real, the members must make some choices.

Another way of looking at resistance is to compare it with what happens in individual counseling or therapy. Most people come into treatment to change and to grow. When insight has been gained and growth seems imminent, the therapist must often shift the major focus of treatment to dealing with the resistance to change and growth. A similar phenomenon occurs in groups. When the group feels that change is imminent, they usually move into a period of resistance.

Resistance is also produced by a fear of dealing with the issues at hand. Any time group members feel threatened by the issue, the process, or the potential solution they defend themselves by incorporating a group defense, the same way an individual uses an individual defense. All the usual individual defenses are available: intellectualization, denial, projection, etc. Members can also call upon defenses that are specific to groups such as pairing, dependency, or scapegoating. We have noticed that some defenses seem more dominant in communities than in other groups.

Communities frequently try to negotiate a contract that doesn't allow the necessary time to achieve their purpose. This a form of resistance. Similarly, they will often negotiate a contract that requires meeting every other week or once a month. This too is a form of resistance. We believe the most successful plan is for groups to meet weekly for a minimum of three months.

Scapegoating is a resistance frequently used by communities. We have described this in greater detail in Chapter 3, but we would like to comment on it further at this point to indicate the specific ways we see it operating in community groups.

God is the most frequently and subtly used scapegoat in a community group. As critical issues begin to surface and feelings begin to rise, someone inevitably starts to speak about God or suggests that the group pray. This is resistance when it uses God to avoid dealing with real human issues.

When conflict began to emerge in one group we worked with, a member who found it difficult immediately suggested that the group break for prayer. Since this is a consistent way of avoiding conflict, we pressured them to stay and confront the issue. When this was successfully completed, we then suggested a period of prayer for reflecting on what they had learned from the experience. They later reported learning that they were controlled by their fantasies of conflict yet were capable of resolving conflict in confronting it directly.

Leaders can be the scapegoats when members become more and more dissatisfied with what is happening in the group. They often blame the leaders for all that is surfacing, as though the leaders have brought it from outside. We have found it helpful to begin our meetings by telling the group that nothing will surface that is not already there and that whatever issue they are avoiding will be even more destructive if they do not deal with it.

One other form of resistance used regularly by community groups is to try to do too much in the course of one meeting. Like everyone else, religious are tired of meetings. There is much truth in the one-liner that describes the spirituality of the 1970s and

1980s: "To Jesus through meetings." Every community would prefer to have as few meetings as possible. But we have discovered that to consider in the same meeting a mixed bag of issues including both ordinary household tasks and improvement of the quality of life is usually ineffectual and frustrating. Separate meetings to handle each issue are more effective in producing satisfactory results.

Role of the Facilitator. The primary responsibilities of group leaders are to create a climate of openness and trust, to facilitate interaction among group members, to keep the group to the task, and to see that they move toward the purpose. We have found the following approaches enhance the effectiveness of community sharing groups.

Be direct—The leaders must have the courage to be constantly direct with the group and to explain what they think is happening. Frequently, leaders don't want to rock the boat or, because of personal fear, prefer to avoid confronting the issue directly.

Be gentle—Since this is a group of people who must live together after the facilitators leave, the leaders must be gentle in

---

RESPONSIBILITIES OF THE FACILITATORS

The Facilitators Must:
Be direct • Feed and Frustrate
Challenge • Serve as consultants
Be gentle • Be sensitive

The Facilitators Must Encourage the Group to:
Reflect prayerfully • Move toward change
Feel potent • Develop open systems
Be realistic • Bring some closure
Face the human issues • Bring out latent content

dealing with the group. The combination of directness and gentleness is probably the most important aspect of leadership in community groups.

Be consultative—The facilitators observe the process that is taking place. As consultants they usually tell the members what they already know but didn't have the courage to admit to one another.

Stop and pray—There are times when emotions are so high that they interfere with the group's ability to listen and communicate effectively. At such times, leaders must suggest that they back off and reflect prayerfully. As mentioned earlier, care must be exercised not to use prayer as a resistance to moving ahead when conflict exists.

Move toward change—Facilitators should help the group constantly to move beyond where it is. The group may learn to communicate well but never achieve its purpose. The leader needs to encourage, prod, and push the group forward.

Help the group to feel potent—One of the major problems with community members is that they frequently feel helpless because they believe they have little control over their lives. Leaders can help them to focus on their strengths and experience their own potency.

Act as a barometer—The group needs to deal with only as much as it can handle in any given session, and it is the facilitators' job to ascertain how much that is. It is important to prevent the group from opening a Pandora's box. This is especially true of groups who must live together during the interval between meetings.

Develop open systems—Community members need to recognize the value of communicating and forming relationships outside the community as well as within the community. When they come to an appreciation and acceptance of this, they are helping one another to differentiate, that is, to grow as individuals. Leaders help communities look at their resistance to creating this open system.

Help the group to be realistic—The leaders should help the group to realize that the only perfect community is an imperfect one. Too many communities spend all their time regretting the past and looking toward the future for an ideal community. Instead, they should be helped to realize that their energies should be directed toward working with the community as it exists now. Only by dealing with their imperfections can the group move toward a more perfect community.

Bring some closure—In consideration of the fact that the group will be living together from one meeting to another, the leaders should help bring enough closure to each meeting that the group members do not go away anxious and unable to talk with one another, yet not so much as to prevent them from reflecting on what has happened.

Face the human issues—The leaders must be willing and able to help the group deal with prefaith issues so that they can recognize their humanness, accept their imperfections, and be willing to work through them as they move toward becoming a faith community. The leaders enable the group to explore the human issues that have prevented them from becoming a stronger faith community.

Bring out the latent content—Frequently, the community will be dealing with only bogus issues. The leader must help to translate what members are saying into what they really mean, so that issues most important to them can be dealt with openly and honestly. We have discussed this more fully in Chapter 3 under scapegoating.

Feed and frustrate—The leaders must be able to sense where the group is at a given time. Sometimes the group members will need to be encouraged and other times they will need to be challenged and even frustrated to get them to do their work.

Members of communities have told us that they feel the least useful approach has been one in which the leaders have followed the sensitivity model—placing people in the hot seat and stripping away their defenses as though they were performing an operation without anesthesia. We have seen the results of this approach when we have been called upon to help put the victims back together after such an experience.

Postgrouping. One approach we have found to be very valuable in working with communities is to end sessions with a ten-minute postgroup session in which we suggest that the members put aside what they have been discussing and begin evaluating how they have worked together, what they have learned from the experience, and how they can improve the quality of their interaction in the future. We find that during this part of the meeting people often share observations and feelings that have been present during the entire meeting but have not been verbalized. A pair of questions that might be used in the postgroup are: Did we accomplish what we set out to do? and How did I experience myself as a member of the group today?

Consultation or Supervision. The use of a supervisor or consultant is intended to assist the leaders in using their skills more effectively. Communities sometimes question whether this use implies a breakdown in confidentiality, or they may interpret supervision as a deficiency or weakness in the facilitator. From our experience supervising group leaders for a number of years, these fears are unfounded. Supervisors or consultants are not interested in the internal workings of the community or in the dynamics of the interpersonal relationships among the members. They look at how accurately the facilitators understand what is happening with the group and how effectively the facilitators are using themselves to help the group move toward its purpose.

Leaders who receive supervision are not deficient but rather are much more likely to keep their personal issues separate from the issues of the group. Each of us has blind spots that can be seen only by another, and persons in helping professions at times need the corrective vision of a supervisor.

One example of this need is a situation in which a priest was working with a community of sisters. At one point in the course of the meetings he became uneasy with what was happening but was unable to identify the cause of his uneasiness. When he brought a tape of a meeting for consultation, it was noticed that at certain times he was giving little homilies. It turned out that the group was using the defense of dependency and he was responding by reverting to a role he felt comfortable with, that of preacher. He was unaware of what was happening until it was pointed out in consultation. After that, whenever he felt a need to preach, he had a better understanding of what was occurring.

Potential Problems with Community Facilitators. We have discovered four potential temptations that often beset community facilitators: (1) They want to make every group a therapy group and fail to recognize that a community sharing group is different. (2) They tend to impose their belief system on a community, a system that often comes from their own experience in community. In short, they try to tell the members how to run their lives. (3) They are not convinced that the community has the ability to be growth producing and that given sufficient time and the proper atmosphere the process will work.

SUMMARY REGARDING FACILITATORS

One thing is evident. There is a great need for well-trained facilitators to assist communities. More and more communities are aware of this need and are seeking qualified and competent facilitators.

As we have indicated earlier, we believe that helping to build community is one of the most necessary ministries in the Church today. Sufficient numbers of persons who have a sophisticated understanding of the workings and dynamics of groups and an appreciation for and understanding of the nature of religious community life must be trained. The uniqueness of community life is something that often escapes those not familiar with the religious community. They fail to understand that communities are really hybrids of many types of groups and have unique characteristics and dynamics. Religious groups supposedly share strong similar goals, and their members often live and work together, thus they have relationships that are in confluence throughout the day. As a group they usually share something of a common history, but they are not brought together by self-selection. Most religious communities are characterized by mobility without having the necessary structures for dealing effectively with the emotional impact of that mobility. For all these reasons, facilitators who work with religious communities need to appreciate the dynamics unique to religious life. Being a well-trained professional group worker, individual therapist, or counselor is not enough.

Religious communities currently have a number of options

available to them. They can hire a facilitator. They can also train members of their own community to act as facilitators. We have seen a number of ways in which communities have trained their own facilitators. Sometimes the local community sends someone to be trained. Another possibility is to train a number of people from the congregation who seem to have a natural talent in this area and either assign them to this ministry in a specified area or region or send them as a team to each area for a prolonged period of time. Whichever method is chosen, the training must be adequate.

CONCLUSION

In this chapter we have provided information for facilitators and offered material that will assist communities to be better educated consumers in obtaining and using facilitators.

VII

Factors That Facilitate Growth in Community

Have you heard the story of the four nuns who lived together in community? To meet and discuss had become a near obsession for them. In spite of all this discussion, there was very little evidence that it led to much action. (Does it sound like a bad case of "barbed wire disease"?) They would talk about the needs of the poor but do little to respond to those needs. They would discuss interminably the role of the religious as lover. At meetings they would wax eloquent on the need for patience, reconciliation, zeal, and all the other Christian virtues, which never appeared to influence their lives together. However, after each of these community meetings, one sister, an elderly woman, would attempt to put the message of the evening's discussion into practice.

Advent came and the nuns decided to make banners reflecting their philosophy and dreams for the community. Each agreed to take the responsibility for making one banner for each Sunday in Advent. They worked diligently and produced some beautiful banners. The first banner read, "They will know we are Christians by our love." The second banner, complete with flowers and butterflies, proclaimed, "Let us love one another in peace and joy."

On the third Sunday, one more beautiful banner was dutifully unfurled with the words, "We embrace the poor like our loving Lord."

Finally, the fourth and last Sunday of Advent arrived. As the sisters entered the chapel for morning prayer, they were greeted by a large banner, made by the elderly, apostolic sister. It declared simply "DAMN IT! DO IT!"

We have now arrived at the "Damn it! do it!" stage of this book. We have offered a great deal of material and now we challenge you to put it into practice in your local community. This book will be a failure if you do not take the initiative to put into practice some of the insights you may have gained from it.

This chapter is both a summary and a synthesis. We will pull together many of the recommendations made in previous chapters and spell out more clearly what you can do to facilitate the quality of life in your own community. We offer the following questions to help you reflect on the appropriate action you can take.

1. *How much do we share faith in our community?* Before you answer this question, reflect on whether you really share faith together in your community or whether you simply come together at the same time, in the same room, to say the same words. To share faith implies something more than what we would usually describe as community prayer. It means allowing someone else to know where, how, and when we have encountered our God. When members of communities are able to share faith they usually grow in love, respect, and trust for one another. Perhaps one of the greatest risks we can take is to share faith with the people we live with, that is, to share the answers to such questions as: When have I been most aware of the presence of God in my life? How do I pray? What is my image of God?

There is a general reluctance among religious to share faith and faith experiences. This is especially true among members of a group living together. Yet we profess that faith is a gift and that this gift is not given for our own benefit but for the building of His Kingdom. Sharing faith is the greatest test of the trust we have in one another. We often seem more willing to share faith and faith experiences with people outside the community than with our immediate group.

**QUESTIONS TO HELP YOU REFLECT ON THE
APPROPRIATE ACTION YOU CAN TAKE**

How much do we share faith in our community?
Do we have a common approach to the apostolate?
Are we able to dialogue on a value level?
How much balance is there in our lives as individuals and as a community?
Can we tolerate being members of an imperfect community?
Do we trust one another enough to risk sharing ourselves?
Do we have clear expectations of one another and the community?
Do we believe in the value of community?
Is our community an open system?

Sharing faith is certainly not a panacea for all the ills in community, but Christian community seems a farce unless we are able to share faith with one another and respect others when they share their faith experiences with us. When we listen to another person share at this level, we come to understand that each of us is truly made in the image and likeness of God. We begin to see the beauty in one another as we listen to others' experiences of encountering and responding to God.

Sharing our faith makes us vulnerable. Dr. Gerald May, a psychiatrist who has been doing research on the drive toward the spiritual experience, discovered that the most difficult thing for people to share is this experience. On one occasion, meeting with a group of psychoanalysts, May discovered that each of them had gone through a true spiritual experience, yet none had talked about it in his or her own analysis. They believed that since they had heard about spiritual experiences and faith so rarely from their own clients, these may actually be foremost among the taboo subjects.

The challenge before each Christian community is to come alive in Christ through sharing on this level. Faith sharing is the foundation of growth as a faith community.

2. *Do we have a common approach to the apostolate?* Some of the best communities we have worked with have really not shared a common approach to the apostolate. What they have shared is their own views of an apostolic approach. The desirable outcome is not so much a common approach as a common vision. Members can accept differences in approach provided there is a oneness of vision. This, of course, implies that what is needed is an openness and willingness to dialogue about visions and approaches to the apostolate. This dialogue is best scheduled at the beginning of the year. Many communities spend days reflecting on and sharing their dreams and hopes for the apostolate and community in the coming year. This is an excellent idea. The community should also plan to evaluate its progress a few months after the initial meeting and again a few months before the end of the year. Too often, communities wait until the end of the year for an evaluation session. This precludes redirecting the group's energy to achieve its objectives.

3. *Are we able to dialogue on a value level?* How often in your community do you take the time to share what you believe, hope for, fear, dream about, and have difficulty with? This is perhaps the most important single factor in developing more successful communities.

Studies that have focused on the relationship between captors and hostages have resulted in interesting insights. When captors and hostages are confined together in a small space, both groups begin to relate to one another as individuals. When this happens there is less chance for the captors to hurt, maim, or kill the hostages because they now know them as persons. How well do we in community know each other as persons? Perhaps we hurt, maim, and kill one another emotionally because we have never gotten to know one another as persons. We have never really dialogued on a value level.

Over and over again in therapeutically treating priests and religious, we have been impressed by the need of these good men and women to share and to dialogue with someone else who will listen to them. They want and need to talk about those things that are of value and importance to them. They have failed to find in community either people or circumstances to facilitate their ability to communicate and share.

In working with communities we have discovered that when the structure permits and encourages a sharing of values, the members of the community readily respond. The structure helps them to overcome their ambivalence, which includes their desire to share and their fear of sharing.

Community meetings are not meant to be soul-baring sessions. They are not sensitivity sessions. They are opportunities for people committed to a common vision to share important issues. We encourage individuals in a community to take the initiative to share with other members and to create a climate in which others might share with them. Special community meetings can be planned in which people have the freedom to talk about their hopes, dreams, fears, and anxieties.

4. *How much balance is there in our lives as individuals and as a community?* Among the most successful communities we have met with is one community of sisters with whom we contracted to meet for twelve sessions on twelve consecutive weeks. At the end of that time both they and we agreed that it wasn't necessary to continue with facilitators. In reviewing what made this community exceptional, we realized that each member received encouragement from the community and seemed to be living a very balanced life. There was time for personal prayer, opportunities to meet and discuss as a community, adequate time to be alone, and some time when the community socialized together. These women were very apostolic. Each was involved in a different ministry and completely committed to that ministry.

A good way to measure the success of your own community is to look at the balance that exists in the lives of the members. Are they people who are fully committed to their apostolates and yet yearn for time to pray alone and at times rejoice to share together?

If the lives of the members are only one or two dimensional, the community life will most likely be boring or tedious. As members enrich their lives, the quality of community life will improve.

5. *Can we tolerate being members of an imperfect community?* A psychiatrist working with Peace Corps volunteers described the stages these people went through. Initially, the volunteers were filled with anxiety and/or enthusiasm. They were usually highly idealistic and had great expectations for what they would discover and accomplish. Inevitably, they soon became disappointed and frustrated. The other people in the Peace Corps were not what they had expected. The system and structure seemed less human than they had anticipated. The work itself did not measure up to their hopes. A parallel can be seen in religious communities. People enter with much enthusiasm and idealism. Soon they discover that the members and the structures of the community are far less than perfect. Their belief in a perfect community consisting of perfect people is soon revealed as a myth. They held the expectation that we should develop a perfect community. In reality the only perfect community is an imperfect one. The true Christian community is one in which we must struggle to understand, accept, and love one another in spite of our differences, our humanity, and our sinfulness.

The successful communities are those in which members are able to accept their imperfections and are willing to work together as they are. In contrast, the less successful communities are those that wait to gather all perfect people before developing community.

We must work at developing community where we find ourselves, realizing and accepting the presence of struggle and frustration. Successful communities accept the differences and idiosyncrasies of the members in a Christian way. Becoming perfect is an ongoing process.

6. *De we trust one another enough to risk sharing ourselves?*

Perhaps the greatest obstacles to developing a faith community are learning to trust one another adequately and growing to believe in the goodness of one another. In Erikson's stages of development he begins with the premise that no development can take place until we are capable of trusting another person.[1] Similarly, no development can occur in communities until we are first able to trust the people with whom we live. To trust them means to believe that they are truly made in the image and likeness of God—that they are good people who have a desire to know, love, and serve God and are capable of accepting and responding to our trust. (Trusting means expecting not to be hurt.)

In his book *Mutual Ministry*, James Fenhagen declares, "We learn to trust those persons with whom we can share our lives. A story-telling ministry is a way of sustaining that community given to us by the spirit. It is a way of enhancing those forces that make for vitality and growth."[2] Sidney Jouard states in *The Transparent Self*, "Self-disclosure is a symptom of personality health and the means of ultimately achieving healthy personality."[3]

We have repeatedly heard religious declare that the people whom they least trusted and with whom they were least able to risk sharing were those they lived with in community. This is a sad commentary on our communal life. We must be willing to risk sharing ourselves with those we live with. Only then can we develop a community in which trust predominates. Only then will we have a community in which the climate contributes to our growth as persons and as a group.

Perhaps the importance of trust has been best clarified by Catherine de Hueck Doherty:

> It is important for us to have faith, trust, confidence in one another. It is the only way we can communicate. Without faith there is no communication, there is no love, or if there was a little love it will die without hope, trust, and confidence. Even if it doesn't die right away, it will be so ill, so weak, and so tired that communication will be miserable as well.
>
> Faith alone can restore communication. Yes, it is time we should believe in one another. It is time we should return to God and ask to be healed from this strange lack of faith, this strange lack of confidence and trust in one another. This is the

moment, this is the hour to turn our faces to God and ask to be healed from the fear of trusting, from the fear of confiding, from the fear of believing in one another.[4]

7. *Do we have clear expectations of one another and of the community?* As we have said earlier, the lack of clarity on expectations interferes with the development of a climate that fosters a healthy community. Clear expectations cannot be developed without dialogue; expectations can never be assumed. In successful communities, members clearly know what they can expect from the community and from its members. Where and in what ways does your community provide the opportunity and structure for this type of dialogue?

8. *Do we believe in the value of community?* In Chapter 1 we delineated our beliefs about the value of community. Ultimately we must all determine for ourselves what value community holds for us, for without an internal, personal conviction that it has value, community life cannot be productive. Do we honestly believe that we can grow more in community than we can in a different situation? Do we believe that community affords us the opportunity to be more effective in using our gifts in ministry? We must all spend time reflecting on the values we see in community and share our thoughts with the members.

9. *Is our community an open system?* A number of years ago, two facilitators led an outpatient therapy group in a mental health center. The leadership alliance worked very effectively and later a request came to them to lead a community group. They decided to do it together, but soon discovered that they were having some difficulty. Through discussion they realized that their approaches differed. One of the leaders was a family systems therapist who firmly believed that to strengthen any system you have to develop and strengthen the individuals. This means fostering the separateness and uniqueness of each person. The other leader discovered that he had been subtly influenced by his past beliefs about community and was attempting to bring people together rather than first helping them to develop as individuals.

As a result of that experience and others, we discovered much about closed and open systems. In general, a closed system is one in which we try to have all of our needs met through one group of people. Closed systems are generally destructive. Religious communities in the past tended to foster and encourage closed systems. We believed that this one group of people with whom we lived should meet all of our needs—spiritual, personal, emotional, and recreational. Healthy communities tend to foster an open system in which some needs are met within the community but others are met outside it.

In evaluating our own community situation, how much do we encourage members to meet some of their needs outside the community? Do we encourage them to have outside friends? Do we encourage them to attend prayer groups occasionally with people other than community members? Do we welcome friends who are not community members?

The ways in which we can foster and encourage a closed system are subtle. We can label people who look outside the community as disloyal when in effect they are really helping the community by enlarging their own lives beyond the confines of the few people they live with.

10. *How much do we affirm others in community?* When we observe something good and commendable in another member, we often seem to have difficulty praising that person for those qualities. More frequently, we confide to another, "Joe is really an edification to me," or "Mary really lives out the ideals of our community in the way she responds to the poor."

Each of us needs to be affirmed. Community is one place where we should legitimately expect to receive affirmation, not only for what we do but also for who we are and for who we are trying to be. Successful communities are affirming communities, places where people directly and openly affirm the good they see in one another.

11. *Can we admit to our own neediness and weakness?* Interestingly, one of the best communities we have observed was in a psychiatric hospital. The concern, care, and love the members of that community had for one another was touching. Perhaps, in their own weakness, they no longer needed to preserve a sense of self-worth by being in competition with one another. They could really allow themselves to be ministered to and in turn could reach out to minister to one another.

QUALITIES WE WOULD LOOK FOR IN A HEALTHY AND SUCCESSFUL COMMUNITY

We can measure the health and maturity of a community by examining the climate that prevails, e.g., is it a climate of tolerance, objectivity, security, and respect? Let us look at each of these characteristics as it applies to the life of the group or community.

Tolerance in Discussion. In a group characterized by tolerance, each member feels free to bring up any idea relevant to the group. There is no fear of destructive criticism, but each member can expect constructive criticism and encouragement. Members listen to one another and ask for clarification if needed to understand another's ideas, plans, and proposals. Members with greater competence contribute more in the area of their competence. Major issues are considered seriously and are given the time needed for discussion, and matters of minor importance are either passed over or relegated to a committee.

When tolerance is lacking, a few people may do all the talking while competent members remain silent. Minor issues get major time and major issues are never discussed.

QUALITIES WE WOULD LOOK FOR IN A HEALTHY AND SUCCESSFUL COMMUNITY
Tolerance in discussion.
Objectivity in decision.
Security in action.
Respect for persons.

Objectivity in Decision. Members of the group are able to put aside judgments based on prejudice or conformity and break with routine in making decisions. Members' ideas are evaluated on merit rather than on how they conform with the usual way of thinking. Decisions are made on the basis of positive facts rather than on sentimentality or abstract ideas. The group can risk experimenting when the facts seem to warrant it.

Security in Action. The group accepts the timing and rhythm of each member's personal maturation and respects individual differences. Members are encouraged to engage in inventive, creative activities. When they experience failure in a new or difficult situation, the group remains supportive. The group engages in long-range planning and is flexible in determining the best means to achieve the objective.

Respect for Persons. The group is aware of its limits and continually evaluates itself through self-criticism, revision, and fraternal correction. Group members work constantly to achieve unity through understanding, mutual support, and love.

CONCLUSION

We return to where we began. We believe that groups have the potential for growth or for destruction and that the direction they take depends primarily on their understanding of the dynamics operating within the group. Since community is a group, it is essential to understand the dynamics at work so that we can move toward constructive growth in community. We hope that as a result of reading this book you have expanded your understanding and knowledge of these dynamics. However, knowledge without action is useless. We must move to the "Damn it! Do it!" stage.

Ultimately, the primary ingredient for making the necessary changes in your community is attitude. Do you believe that your God is a good God who has placed you in community because He believes you will grow to your fullness there? That you as an individual have the ability to grow within community life? That the others you are living with are good people, capable of assisting you in that growth? That community is and can be a place where real growth is stimulated for you and for others? Do you believe that your call to fullness of life in Christ can be achieved inside Christian community?

NOTES

1. Eric Erikson, *Childhood and Society* (New York: Norton and Co., 1963) pp. 247–251.
2. James Fenhagen, *Mutual Ministry* (New York: Seabury Press, 1977), p. 41.
3. Sidney Jourard, *The Transparent Self* (Princeton: Van Nostrand, 1964), p. 32.
4. Catherine de Hueck Doherty, *Poustinia: Christian Spirituality of the East for Western Man* (Notre Dame, Ind.: Ave Maria, 1975), p. 151 f.

Appendix

Experiencing Termination
in Community

Group theorists maintain that all groups move through predictable stages. Although the phases of group structure and the formal labels attached to the stages of group life vary according to specific theories, there is an indisputable common element. Inevitably, any group will experience termination—no group exists in perpetuum. Whether one individual separates from the group or the group itself ceases to exist, termination will occur.

Community life is a group experience and as such is not exempt from the processes underlying all groups. When the community gathers for the first time, it begins its group life together. At some point in its history (whether the time is brief or extended) the composition of the community will change.

A single member of a group may leave while the rest of the members remain, but this one loss terminates the identity of this particular group. When the community resumes with a different membership constellation, it is a new and different group, and the cycle begins anew.

It is our belief that termination exerts a profound impact on the lives of community members, yet it is a little recognized or understood dynamic. Formation programs prepare individuals for many aspects of community life but rarely for dealing with this experience.

Reprinted from *Human Development*, Summer 1981.

Termination, which involves a separation that frequently produces painful feelings of loss, affects individuals in two basic ways: as a real loss in the present and as a catalyst and symbol for bringing to the surface the unresolved feelings connected with terminations experienced in the past.

TERMINATION AS LOSS IN THE PRESENT

Pause for a few moments and recall a community in which you lived or an apostolate in which you ministered, where you grew very close to those with whom you lived or worked. Remember the feelings that surrounded that experience and the special place those people had in your life. When you have spent some time cherishing memories, try to recollect the feelings and the intense emotions that were generated when you left. In all probability such a separation produced a profound sense of loss accompanied by feelings of intense sadness, pain, and emptiness. Ask yourself these questions: How did I deal with those feelings? With whom did I share them? Did I allow the other parties involved to share and discuss their feelings?

Our experience in working with members of religious communities is that individuals not only avoid dealing with the feelings surrounding separation but they also tend to deny or suppress them. It is regrettable that there are members of religious communities who have remained on the periphery and have never experienced the pain of separation and termination. They never invest themselves enough to become close to others and to develop a sense of intimacy, a quality that frees a person to share with another without fear of rejection or loss of self-identity. According to psychoanalyst Erik Erikson's theory of development, a person cannot exhibit concern for society or guide future generations (generativity) until he has resolved the crises surrounding relationships (intimacy). It is difficult to believe that religious who have shielded themselves from the vulnerability of intimacy can be truly ministering people capable of being and doing for others.

STAGES OF TERMINATION

Elisabeth Kübler-Ross's classic work on death and dying provides a model for the dynamics that occur when an individual experiences termination of a meaningful relationship. She has enumerated five stages through which people generally proceed: denial, anger, bargaining, depression, and finally, acceptance. There are parallel dynamics for religious who experience termination from a community or ministry.

Initially, there is a denial of the loss, or a denial of the feelings generated by the loss. Many religious have labeled feelings as bad and therefore work hard to deny them. If, for example, Brother Joe feels sadness at the time of termination, he might struggle to deny (unconsciously) that feeling for fear that shedding tears would be seen as a lack of virility. In doing so, he denies a very basic, beautiful emotion. He denies that the loss has meaning for him. Like many male religious, he may resort to humor in an attempt to hide the intense feelings that make him very uncomfortable.

At the second stage, denied feelings are expressed as anger. Illogical as it may seem, this anger may be directed toward those we will miss. More often it will be directed at others who become innocent victims of our displaced anger. At times of termination we often see a great deal of free-floating hostility. For example, Sister Mary is being reassigned to a new convent and ministry after years of dedicated, loving ministry among a group of Hispanic parishioners. During her years there, a beautiful bond of mutual love has developed between her and the parishioners. She experiences pain in anticipating the termination and separation and expresses it in outbursts of anger toward the young curate. Everything he does is wrong. She is also critical of everything that is happening in the community and berates the young sisters for their lack of commitment. She is what some would describe as an "angry woman." In reality, she is a hurting woman. Her hurt is being felt as anger and expressed as hostility. As destructive as this might be, it is better than what frequently occurs. Many religious, like Brother Joe, deny their feelings. But denied feelings must be expressed in some way. When anger is repressed (unconsciously) or suppressed (consciously), it is often turned inward. Sister Mary may become depressed as her anger is turned inward. It is a very real, honest response to a painful situation, an anticipated termination. The difficulty is not with the feeling but with the way it is being expressed.

A bargaining process that is an attempt to work out an arrangement that will alleviate the finality of the termination is the next

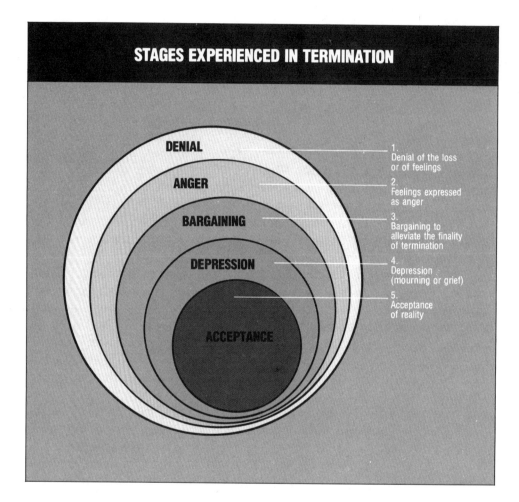

stage. Father Tom has been involved in a process of discerning for the past year. He has reached a point where he is questioning his effectiveness in his ministry as a high school teacher. He begins searching for a new ministry, but one that allows him to continue teaching on a part-time basis. He seeks a way of terminating a ministry in which he no longer feels effective, but at the same time he is ambivalent and wants to soften the finality of the decision by not letting go. He has reached the stage that has been described as the time "to stop discerning and start deciding." To leave this apostolate that has given him so much satisfaction in the past will be very difficult. To hold on to it when he knows he is not being effective is potentially destructive for him and for his students.

As we enter into mourning and grief, the feeling of depression follows. Depression is a normal, healthy consequence of loss. Brother Joe, Sister Mary, and Father Tom simply have to accept this as a normal process in the life of a "pilgrim person." Some degree of depression is inevitable, but it can be the source of a new life of resurrection if we accept it, confront it, work through it, and reinvest ourselves as people of faith in the beauty of the new life. In the healthy personality, there is a gradual acceptance and reinvestment of the self in new people and new situations.

Termination of a meaningful relationship produces stress. The degree and intensity of loss experienced is in proportion to the depth and meaning of the relationship. Mental health professionals have long been aware that the most traumatic experiences that a person must endure are often those involving termination and separation. In this day and age, when stress and burnout have become so commonplace, religious communities must be more aware of the impact that loss and termination have on their members. Failure to recognize and respond to this situation can only have a profoundly negative impact on the lives of the persons affected and render them less effective as the ministering people the Lord has called them to be.

TERMINATION AS SYMBOLIC

Loss is always two dimensional. Not only do we experience the pain of the present loss, but each loss, no matter how insignificant, serves as a catalyst for bringing unresolved feelings to the surface. It brings to the forefront of our psyche suppressed or repressed feelings surrounding previous terminations, particularly those we have avoided facing or have not adequately resolved. The present loss serves as a symbol to "re-present" the unfinished grieving of intense past losses. Grieving is never completed; there is always a certain amount left unfinished.

Recall an event in your life in which you experienced a loss that was seemingly minor yet provoked a reaction that was intense and out of proportion to the event that precipitated it. You may have been puzzled by the amount of grief generated by this relatively minor loss. This new loss was serving as a stimulus and vehicle for releasing unfinished business from the past.

A good example of this kind of catalytic event can be seen in the story shared by a friend. He had just viewed the poignant movie *The Way We Were*, left the theater, and returned to his car. Suddenly and quite unexpectedly he found himself affected by the movie. His mind worked like a slide projector as each of the profound losses he had experienced in his life resurfaced. The movie had served as a catalyst for releasing some of the still-unfinished grieving, and he found himself weeping.

We have seen communities in which the death of a pet has produced grief far beyond what would seem normal. What we are witnessing is a true, symbolic termination. The death of the dog or cat has allowed people to release some of the pain and grief they did not allow themselves to experience at the time of an earlier, more meaningful loss. The memory and pain that accompanied the death of a parent when religious life disapproved of outward expression of feelings may be revived. Perhaps the barrier to expression was the personal expectations that a religious placed on himself, the series of "shoulds" that have dictated his life: "I should be strong." "I should be a minister to the others in my family." "I should be a good example of the tower of strength (or the valiant woman) to the others in my family." Whatever the "shoulds" were that prevailed in the example of the pet, the earlier grief was buried and then released by another, less traumatic loss. The pet's death becomes the outlet for the grieving that was never before accomplished.

TERMINATION AS A DEVELOPMENTAL PROCESS

One of the reasons why termination is such a powerful dynamic in our lives is related to our individual development. Human development is a series of terminations and separations, each of which provides a point of great trauma in the development of the individual.

The process begins at birth when the infant is separated from its mother's womb. As the young child grows and develops a sense of independence, the work of identifying himself or herself as a separate and unique individual begins. Throughout adolescence and into young adulthood, the individual gradually relinquishes emotional supports and separates from the guardianship of the family. The adult years are checkered with numerous separations of varying significance as the person moves toward the fear of the ultimate separation in life—death. None of these transitions is ever perfectly resolved. In our progress through these stages the "unfinished" crises continue to influence our present life, and we try to resolve them as we encounter new separations and terminations. Some therapists maintain that the most therapeutic moments in people's lives are those when they successfully work through a separation and termination. Some therapies even focus on forcing people to deal with the reality of such endings.

TERMINATION IN COMMUNITY

Termination is a powerful dynamic in the lives of religious, yet religious tend to ignore its impact on community life. In responding to apostolic or congregational needs, the religious is frequently "on the move." Rarely does a religious live with the same community for an extended length of time. Even if the individual remains, one or several other community members will depart. A religious community that does not experience a yearly change in membership is probably the exception rather than the rule. Religious, whether they are the persons leaving or those staying behind, encounter separation on a regular basis, and each separation involves terminations of relationships of those who have lived and labored together.

The effects of termination have great repercussions on community life, yet these are frequently ignored. For the young religious, separation, especially from peers leaving religious life, has a profound impact. Communities fail to provide opportunities for a young person to discuss these feelings and even discourage such discussion. This may result in a fight or flight reaction on the part of the young person. Fearing the hurt involved in establishing friendships, individuals isolate themselves from community and become more individualistic. At the other extreme, they may react in anger, expressing hostility toward a convenient scapegoat, which is frequently the administration.

At the opposite end of the spectrum are the older religious who encounter frequent deaths of close friends, family members, and peers. These religious are forced to grapple with the reality of their own impending death. Even for a man or woman of faith, this can provoke anxiety.

Religious in their midyears often experience the trauma of constant uprooting. This situation parallels what is occurring in society at large. Statistics indicate that 25% of all Americans move every year. Usually, when a man or woman relocates, the family that provides emotional and psychological support also moves. This is generally not the case for religious. When the religious relocates to another ministry, community, or geographic area, the Christian community he worked with, or the local religious community that provided a source of support, is left behind, and this adds to the difficulty of transition. Many religious have likened the situation to divorce with all its inherent trauma. Transition may be felt even more acutely by religious who see their friends sinking roots at the very time their own uprootedness is becoming more difficult and a standard way of life for religious.

In the last few years we have encountered a number of religious who are unable to reinvest themselves in new assignments. They describe themselves as having no energy left, nothing more to give. Community life and ministry are putting demands on individuals that seem to drain their strength and to accentuate their lack of zeal, a condition popularly referred to as burnout. Closer investigation of such an individual provides a picture of a person who has invested himself deeply in relationships and in ministries and has experienced a series of terminations. The specific details delineate a loving, committed person who generously gives of himself to others, but who lacks a realization of the emotional toll that terminations produce. By avoiding the feelings concomitant with separation, people on their way to burnout cannot experience any sense of closure. They become one-dimensional pilgrims, always moving on, but leaving a part of themselves behind. After a series of transitions that have not been worked through, there is nothing left to give, and they experience a profound sense of emptiness.

But religious *are* pilgrims. And as pilgrim people we must be ready to move on and so must make a special effort to take with us in our hearts those we leave behind. After resolving some of our feelings about separation, we can reinvest ourselves with renewed vigor and commitment. The pain of loss still exists, but the memory of the beauty of the relationships give us a sense of joy and gratitude.

GOODBYE BEFORE HELLO

Experience in religious communities often reveals that the group cannot allow new people into it until it has adequately relinquished the former members; the group members cannot say hello until they have learned to say goodbye. We visited a large city parish recently that had a greatly loved pastor, a member of a religious community. When he was transferred, he claimed that the people would not be able to deal effectively with his absence. He managed, as is quite evident, to project his own difficulty with termination onto the parishioners. As a result, he did not tell the parishioners he was leaving until the Sunday before his departure. They experienced a mixture of sorrow and hurt—and anger. Their problem was to determine the object of their anger. They loved the pastor too much to be angry with him. The religious superiors who transferred the man were too far away for the parishioners to express their anger toward them. So, as frequently happens, the new pastor was the recipient of the anger. It took the people a couple of years before they accepted this man, because his predecessor never allowed the people to express their sadness, hurt, and anger toward him for leaving them.

Similarly, in communities, we are often unable to incorporate new members because we have not yet adequately dealt with our feelings toward those who have left. This is likely to happen when those who left meant a lot to us, and especially if they initiated the change.

Living community life today places the religious in a stress-filled dilemma. A community that involves sharing and growing in intimacy is strongly advocated, but rarely are opportunities provided for religious to deal adequately with the pain of loss that this type of community life engenders.

There is an increasing sensitivity to the pain and needs of the individual who is departing, but there is no corresponding awareness of the pain in store for those who remain. The person leaving can enjoy the excitement and anticipation of a new experience; those who are left behind often feel only a sense of loss and emptiness. Consequently, termination is usually more difficult for those who remain, and communities must be much more sensitive to this group's plight.

In her book *Unfinished Business*, Maggie Scarf states that according to recent research, termination is more traumatic for women than for men, because women generally invest themselves more intensely in relationships than do men. The result of such intensity is that women experience separations and terminations with a sense of devastation that often leads to depression. Communities of women, especially, must provide their members with explicit opportunities to deal with terminations.

It is not the purpose of this article to advocate avoiding terminations. They are inevitable, and it is our belief that they provide opportunities for personal growth. A few religious will be too psychologically weak to withstand frequent terminations, yet the majority of religious possess the emotional and psychological strength to tolerate them. Dealing with feelings generated by termination does not lessen the pain involved; instead, the pain gives birth to new insights and strengthens our emotional health. Successful confrontation of the feelings allows us to grow in the zest and excitement vital to living full personal and ministerial lives. Key questions in the life of a religious must be, How do I deal with termination? What can I learn? Is there room for growth or change?

DEALING WITH TERMINATION

Although religious profess to be death-resurrection people, this perception more frequently reflects rhetoric than reality. In community life, religious have avoided dealing with the death, the terminations and separations, and have proceeded directly to the resurrection. Community life is unreal if the normal, slow process of moving through death to resurrection is absent. To live in community is to experience a rhythm of light and darkness, a test of faith and doubt, and an emergence of love and loneliness. Movement from death to resurrection demands active participation. Religious must not be passive victims of termination. To avoid this, we suggest the following:

Attempt to isolate and identify feelings. The feelings associated with termination are many and varied. They are influenced not only by our personal, unique past but also by the level of intimacy in the relationship. One consistent feeling present at termination is ambivalence (the coexistence of positive and negative feelings toward the same person, object, or event). An example is the experience at graduation. The joyful anticipation of what lies ahead is mixed with sadness in leaving behind familiar persons, places, and situations.

Don't flee from feelings. When you experience the pain of termination, take time to reflect on it. Because of the pain involved, we often settle for a conscious awareness of only the most superficial feelings. The more open you can be, the more opportunities you have to grow in the experience.

Accept each of the feelings as appropriate. Terminations may bring feelings of relief, anger, sadness, anxiety, joy, or any combination of a myriad of feelings. None are wrong. Feelings are simply a response to stimuli. Many religious have developed sensitive radar systems that allow them to be supportive and encourage others to accept their feelings while maintaining a strict self-censorship of their own. Whatever feelings are generated by termination must be accepted without condemning ourselves for their inappropriateness.

Each of us has consciously learned a list of feelings that we believe are inappropriate for or unacceptable to us. When these feelings are aroused and we refuse to acknowledge them consciously, they are often expressed in inappropriate behavior. Anger, for instance, has been labeled by Brother John as an inappropriate feeling for a minister. Instead of dealing with legitimate anger, he unconsciously stores it in his personal pressure cooker where it is likely to explode one day at the wrong person or at the wrong time, with an intensity disproportional to the precipitating event. When we can accept the feeling, we can choose to deal with it in a mature, appropriate manner.

Talk about your feelings. This is the most important aspect of the process and frequently the point at which the process becomes short-circuited. Few religious have been trained to discuss feelings, and to verbalize them can be an intimidating prospect. Yet is is imperative that these feelings be talked about, especially among persons sharing the termination. This dialogue should be anticipated long before the last farewells; to relegate it to the final meeting defeats the purpose. Individuals need time to get in touch with and work through feelings. Thus, the dialogue should be initiated several weeks before the actual ending to allow for closure.

Secrecy and ambiguity breed anxiety, yet some communities still maintain a system of changes that perpetuates rumor and counter-rumor. The less this occurs and the more the community can be involved in the process of decision making surrounding the change, the healthier the results will be for the individual and for the community.

Sharing is most beneficial when the dialogue is honest and direct.

This level of interaction indicates trust in those we share with; it also involves personal risk. Discussing personal feelings with another places us in a vulnerable position. When a community respects the individual's willingness to take a risk, an atmosphere of support is created and this, in turn, may encourage others to disclose their feelings.

It is important to state again at this point that both the person leaving and the people left behind experience a sense of loss. All those involved must be encouraged to talk about their feelings. When this dialogue takes place, termination can be one of the most enriching experiences in community life.

A personal story that was related to us perhaps best describes how this can be done:

> I can recall very vividly my change from a community and a ministry which had been a beautiful and rewarding experience. Leaving was very difficult for me. The other members of the community shared honestly and openly their feelings about my leaving and permitted me to do the same. I can remember one instance in particular. One of my confreres, who was not ordinarily seen as a sensitive person, approached me and shared quite simply and beautifully what he felt I had meant to the community and that I would be greatly missed. I left the encounter with a deep sense of appreciation to that man, as well as very moist eyes.

If each of us were willing to engage in this type of dialogue, we would certainly find terminations an experience that fosters growth in our holiness and healthiness.

Allow the others involved to talk about their feelings. The most difficult step in the termination process is to listen to another's pain, since listening arouses our own present grief and triggers unresolved griefs of the past. This can be a threatening experience. Our normal tendency is to avoid the issue and to quickly change the topic of conversation.

Since it is difficult to speak directly about terminations, the message frequently comes to us disguised, and we can easily miss it. In general, people talk about feelings of loss in symbolic ways. Topics such as death and sickness can become obsessive themes in groups experiencing termination. At this juncture communities may need the assistance of a facilitator who can assist the group in translating the symbolic language. Communities seem to enter into an unspoken collusion to avoid discussing the feelings associated with termination. An example can be seen in a situation in which we served as facilitators for a community of men. During their final session all the traditional themes emerged. They were unable to stick to the agenda and tasks they had defined. Instead, there followed a litany of "can-you-top-this" stories of recent sicknesses and deaths. As cofacilitators of the group, we attempted to point out that they were off the track. It was apparent that their need to talk about the termination themes without addressing their feelings was strongly ingrained. Our initial attempts to point this out were met with denial and resistance, which was followed by discussion of other termination themes. Finally, our repeated interventions were successful and the group, with a sense of relief, began talking directly about their feelings. As a result, they experienced a great deal of personal growth, and they accomplished the difficult task of dealing directly with termination, something they had never previously been able to do.

If the feelings surrounding termination are not addressed directly or symbolically, they may erupt in bizarre, regressive behavior. In our experience, we have witnessed such behavior in groups of otherwise mature individuals, with the fight or flight themes being expressed in extreme forms. Often, it appears that groups that have been growing toward their goal of being stronger faith communities regressively manifest the type of polarization and hostility that dominated their earlier meetings. It is as though they are trying to convince themselves that they really haven't progressed that far and that it is futile to attempt to do so. At this stage the facilitator faces the difficult task of helping the group to see that the regression and resistance represent a normal fear of dealing with termination.

The other major form of resistance employed by communities to avoid dealing with termination is to cancel the last few meetings because "we're all too busy."

Ritualize the loss. For the process to be completed, termination needs to be ritualized. Our society formalizes certain key passages in life. For example, the bar mitzvah marks a young man's departure from childhood into manhood; a woman's bridal shower celebrates her entrance into a new state of life; and the office retirement party formally closes the door on many years of labor. Often, religious communities celebrate the end of the year but do not make it explicit that the celebration marks the end of the community. It is important that ritualization be accompanied by dialogue about the termination. Both are essential. The ritualization can take the form of a liturgy, party, or any other form that allows the community to symbolically relate to its ending.

Allow yourself the time and space to grieve. Death, when it comes suddenly, brings the most poignant experience of grief; its irrevocableness deprives us of the gradual process of termination. This abrupt end to a meaningful relationship leaves us with a feeling of incompleteness and impotency. Perhaps these feelings are capsuled in the reaction of a woman who, on learning of the sudden death of her father, could only cry helplessly, "But I didn't say goodbye."

Similarly, some degree of grief and sense of incompleteness accompany all terminations. When religious communities end their life together as a group, the individual members are likely to feel sad. Since grieving is absolutely essential to complete the unfinished business of termination, it is important to allow sufficient time for it. Grieving follows its own pattern and timetable; you cannot program it. There is no need to say "but I should be finished grieving by now."

Reinvest yourself in new relationships and situations. This is the culmination of the death-resurrection process. Allowing ourselves to progress through the phases of separation and loss revitalizes and integrates us. As we release our grasp on the past, we become free to embrace new relationships and new situations. We have met the Lord in those we have lived with and ministered to. We are grateful, but it is time to move on to discover him anew in others. This is the ultimate sign of health and maturity: to have progressed through the slow process of grieving to the point at which we are prepared to risk investing ourselves in new relationships.

GRIEVING CAN LIBERATE

Termination is an inevitable stage in the life of every community. It can be a painful process that we resist because of the feelings it generates. Sometimes the pain will be directly related to the present loss. At other times it may be the result of unfinished business from long-past terminations.

Ultimately, as people of hope, we must allow ourselves to proceed through the slow, often painful process of normal grieving, with all its component parts. Terminations dealt with leave us free to reinvest ourselves in people and situations where we can again encounter the Lord.

RECOMMENDED READING

Bowlby, John. *Loss.* New York: Basic Books, 1981.

Bowlby, John. *Separation.* New York: Basic Books, 1973.

Feinberg, Mortimer, Gloria Feinberg, and John Tarrant. *Leavetaking.* New York: Simon and Schuster, 1978.

Kübler-Ross, Elisabeth. *On Death and Dying.* New York: Macmillan & Co., 1969.

Bibliography

Clark, Stephen, *Building Christian Communities*, Notre Dame, Ind.: Ave Maria Press, 1973.

Hammett, Rosine, Sofield, Loughlan, "Some Reflections on Confidentiality," *Sisters Today,* Vol. 51, No. 3, November 1979.

Meissner, William, *Group Dynamics in the Religious Life*, Indiana: University of Notre Dame Press, 1965.

Ohlsen, Merle, *Group Counseling*, New York: Holt, Rinehart and Winston, 1970.

Rubin, Jesse, "The Group Network," *Group Studies Journal*, Vol. 1, No. 1, 1973.

Scarff, Maggie, *Unfinished Business: Pressure Points in the Lives of Women*, New York: Doubleday, 1980.

Sofield, Loughlan, Hammett, Rosine, "Experiencing Termination in Community," *Human Development*, Summer 1981.

Vanier, Jean, *Community and Growth: Our Pilgrimage Together*, New York: Paulist Press, 1979.

Yalom, Irving, *The Theory and Practice of Group Psychotherapy*, New York: Basic Books, 1970.